AF684738

Workbooks for Psychotherapists

Volume I:

Understanding Unconscious Communication

The Workbook Series . . .
by Robert Langs, M.D.

WORKBOOKS FOR PSYCHOTHERAPISTS

Volume I:
Understanding Unconscious Communication

Volume II:
Listening and Formulating

Volume III:
Intervening and Validating

Workbooks for Psychotherapists

Volume I:
Understanding Unconscious Communication

Robert Langs, M.D.

NEWCONCEPT press, inc.
EMERSON, NEW JERSEY

To Elise...
and the vibrancy
of communication

Copyright © 1985 by Newconcept Press, Inc.

All rights reserved. No part of this book may be reproduced in any form, by photostat, microform, retrieval system, or any other means, without the prior written permission of the publisher.

NEWCONCEPT PRESS, INC.
EMERSON, NEW JERSEY 07630

Library of Congress
Catalog Card Number
84—62354

ISBN 0-931231-01-9

Printed in the United States of America
10 9 8 7 6 5 4 3

Contents

Preface

This volume is the first in a series of workbooks designed to enable readers to participate actively in learning how to do psychotherapy. Because all sound and insightful therapy depends on a reliable use of the listening process, this first volume is designed to focus on the most essential dimension of listening in psychotherapy: understanding and decoding the patient's unconscious expressions. It is this effort that gives access to the patient's unconscious meanings as they express and illuminate his or her psychopathology. Such efforts are therefore fundamental to understanding the unconscious basis of madness. I am using the term *madness* to designate all forms of emotionally-founded dysfunctions because, unlike words such as insanity or mental illness, for example, the term madness can be used inclusively, to indicate both an inner mental disturbance and its outer manifestations in thought, behaviors, and feelings.

As a workbook, this volume offers brief discussions on different aspects of psychotherapeutic listening, along with a series of practical exercises designed to engage the reader in the process of understanding and decoding patient productions. Space is provided within the book for answers to the questions posed in the exercises, and the author's suggested responses are given directly afterward. This strategy has been adopted in the hope that active participation in the somewhat compressed and yet readily mastered decoding process will facilitate familiarity with and sensitive use of this fundamental therapeutic tool.

The reader who is interested in background reading on the technique of psychoanalytic psychotherapy should refer to *Psychotherapy: A Basic Text* (Langs, 1982) for backup support as needed. The present book, however, is self-contained and can be read through on its own. Because this volume deals primarily with issues of communication in the therapeutic setting, I establish, throughout, aspects of the interplay between intrapsychic formulations and a communicative approach to patient expressions as vehicles of messages, both within and outside of a patient's conscious awareness.

I have written intermittently on the listening process for over ten years. It is tribute to the complexities of human communication—especially to communication within the therapeutic interaction—that the achievement of fresh discoveries and new insights continues in this area. Thus, although the present volume reflects and, indeed, is based on my prior work on listening and interpretation (see in particular Langs, 1983), it is also a vehicle for new understanding. Its main purpose is to enable psychotherapists to master a fundamental tool necessary for sound insight psychotherapy: the decoding of the patient's encoded messages, the only access to the true meaning of unconscious communication.

Robert Langs, M.D.
New York City

1 Unconscious Communication and Madness

INTRODUCTION

There are many factors contributing to emotional dysfunction, or madness, in human beings, patients and therapists alike. By madness I mean all types of emotional disorders: psychotic, neurotic, narcissistic, characterological, somatic, and otherwise. Of the factors that might be considered—social and cultural, biological and psychobiological, intrapsychic and interpersonal, the influence of fantasy and perception, individual and family history, and so on—psychoanalysis, along with its offspring, psychoanalytic psychotherapy, has concerned itself largely with the intrapsychic and interpersonal dimensions of madness. In this workbook I do not distinguish between these two treatment modalities, because the ideas and tools presented apply to both psychoanalysis and psychoanalytic psychotherapy with comparable pertinence. Psychoanalysis has sought to provide patients relief from emotional suffering primarily by establishing a secure framework for the treatment experience and a sound holding and containing relationship with the therapist; by dictating that the therapist respond to the behaviors and associations of the patient with silences, interpretations, reconstructions, and framework-management responses; and by implicitly fostering in the patient an inevitable unconscious introjective identification with the well-functioning therapist.

Each of these components of cure are dependent on one another. In particular, a sound holding relationship must be supported, when necessary, by interventions that secure the framework and by validated interpretive and reconstructive work. Conversely, the constructive influence of a confirmed interpretation, which leads to intrapsychic-conflict resolution and development of adaptive resources, must be supported by a healthy therapeutic symbiosis—the ideal frame and mode of relatedness for the psychotherapeutic experience.

Fundamental to the psychoanalytic therapeutic endeavor is a recognition of the importance of *unconscious factors* in all forms of madness. Other contributing causes notwithstanding, an extremely important component of emotional dysfunction exists entirely outside the awareness of the patient, finding expression only in disguised or encoded form. The patient may lack conscious realization not only of the influence of repressed genetic and other experiences, but of the meanings and functions of his or her immediate associations and behaviors. Those who practice psychoanalysis and psychoanalytic psychotherapy contend that, given the ego support provided a patient by a sound holding and containing relationship (the basis of a healthy therapeutic symbiosis), the specific insight afforded to a patient, based on the validated interpretation of his or her material, will lead to a variety of constructive consequences—among others, conflict resolution, interpersonal change, intrapsychic structural realignment, self-enhancement, the development of new adaptive resources, and true growth. These will gradually create a highly durable, adaptive resolution to a patient's emotional disorder. Although there are, indeed, other means by which patients obtain relief from madness, such therapists claim that insight into the meaning of unconscious material is the most proficient and least damaging or constricting means by which emotional disturbances may be resolved.

At the heart of the psychoanalytic therapeutic technique, then, is an understanding of the patient's *unconscious communications*—his or her encoded, or disguised messages. It is therefore essential for a therapist to appreciate and to be capable of fully applying the kind of listening process whereby a patient's unconscious expressions can be properly decoded and understood for their most cogent meanings and functions. For many years now, psychoanalysts have believed that they share in common a listening process of this kind. As documented elsewhere (Langs, 1981a), however, extensive evidence indicates that this is not the case. It therefore behooves us, experienced analyst and novice alike, to study the nature of unconscious communication and to perfect, as far as is possible, the means by which encoded messages can be properly and incisively decoded. This workbook is a contribution to that end.

SOME BASIC MODELS

In his greatest work, *The Interpretation of Dreams* (1900), Freud, in a moment of singular insight, proposed that human mentation takes two basic forms: what he called primary-process and secondary-process thinking. Secondary-process thinking is conscious thinking; it is attuned to the external world and proceeds by way of individual, discrete thoughts. These thoughts are logical, sequential, and confined to manifest meaning. Primary-process thinking occurs mainly by way of narratives and visual images that have multiple meanings. Such thinking is fluid and unconcerned with objective reality or sequential time. It readily shifts about without linear focus, and uses a set of specific and unique mechanisms in its operation.

Freud's basis for working out the laws of primary-process mentation was the reported dream. Freud believed that memories and fantasies which are ordinarily repressed from consciousness gain access to consciousness during dreams, when defenses are relaxed. In order to experience these threatening images without anxiety, the dreamer unconsciously transforms them, by way of primary-process mentation, into less threatening verbal and visual equivalents. When the dreamer reports the dream, these transformed images are pulled into a secondary-process narrative that gives them an immediate surface meaning; but they also contain evidence of the threatening repressed thoughts from which they are derived. These repressed thoughts are said to be "latent" in the disguised images; they have been permitted conscious expression, but they remain unconscious to the person telling the dream.

Freud was interested in the means by which an anxiety-provoking memory or fantasy is transformed into a manifest dream element, and conversely, how a manifest dream could be decoded into its latent meanings. The discovery of the mechanisms of transformation would indicate those processes that had to be undone or reversed in order to decipher the manifest dream elements.

The Depth Model

Freud's original idea about intrapsychic functioning was that repressed mental contents seeking access to consciousness are kept at bay by a repressing force. The model he used to illustrate his hypothesis (the topographic model, presented in *The Interpretation of Dreams*) is now mainly discarded, but its physical imagery continues to shape the ideas of psychotherapists today. The model for intrapsychic functioning is generally that of a surface which in some way reveals but also conceals a configuration lying deeper, on a lower psychic stratus. This is why psychoanalysis has been called a depth psychology. Sometimes the image envisioned is that of an opaque surface lying above contents hidden within the depths, accessible only via some type of fresh opening.

This model is not without value. It has stood the test of time, because it has helped psychotherapists to visualize the idea that unconscious factors contribute to surface madness. Nevertheless, the value of any psychological or dynamic model is limited by the concrete nature of its imagery, which ultimately misleads. The depth model encourages the reification of what is mistakenly called "the unconscious," in that the model suggests a static state of affairs rather than a continual interplay of dynamic forces. The model leads to notions of fixed elements pressing upward, seeking discharge, and to the sense that these elements involve isolated or concrete thoughts or ideas.

The depth model, accordingly, has had important technical consequences for the practice of psychotherapy. It leads to digging by the psychotherapist, to probing, to "penetrating" questions, to pushing past a surface association by asking the patient to move deeper, to go further, or to somehow pull out in direct and manifest form the deeper, hidden contents of the unconscious mind. The endeavor is directed toward reaching in and gaining access to an emergent disguised unconscious element. A great deal of psychoanalytic listening and technique has been designed in this fashion. The model leads to much active probing by the psychotherapist and to a belief that those associations which the patient produces in response to this probing tend to embody the underlying concealed contents.

It is critical in examining this model to recognize the absence of a postulated process of transformation and disguise. Despite Freud's consideration of these mechanisms in *The Interpretation of Dreams* (1900), the model of listening used by many psychotherapists is entirely devoid of reference to a need to undo disguise or decipher transformed images. The unconscious element is expected to leap whole cloth through the opening provided by the probes of the psychotherapist, and once stated directly, its supposed unconscious meaning is presumed to have been captured. However, there is considerable evidence to indicate that unconscious material does not reach the surface of the patient's associations in this manner, so that the depth model of psychoanalysis has ultimately proved as misleading as it has been helpful.

It is this concern about the reification of psychoanalytic terms, including such questionable ideas as "the unconscious mind" that has led Schafer (1976) to propose a new language for psychoanalysis—a language that refers to a patient's behaviors rather than to psychic functioning. A related and alternative resolution of these issues is the *communicative approach*, in which the emphasis is placed not on the mind and mentation but, rather, on conscious and unconscious expressions—communication. Such an approach is capable both of dealing with intrapsychic, interpersonal, and interactional factors in emotional dysfunctions and also of generating a revised model of the unconscious dimension of human madness.

The Communicative Approach to Madness

Stimulus and Adaptive Response. The development of madness may be understood in terms of a simple stimulus-response paradigm. In general, we may propose that traumatic stimuli may lead to the maladaptive responses that we term emotional dysfunctions, or madness. Symptoms and interpersonal dysfunctions are only one kind of response among the many responses to a stimulus that are possible; when these symptoms and dysfunctions do appear, however, their unconscious structure proves to be of great importance. By the word *unconscious* I mean those aspects of a stimulus that lie outside the awareness of the sender (the creator of of the stimulus), the receiver, or both; but nonetheless induce in the receiver a tendency to respond. The unconscious aspects of messages sent and received and the responses to these messages are crucial in the development of an emotional disturbance and in the perpetuation of symptoms indicating that disturbance. Because they exist outside the awareness of the individual experiencing the symptoms, such unconscious factors *cannot be stated directly* by that individual; they can be expressed only indirectly—through messages *derived* from those unconscious factors, but *symbolized* by mental contents that are conscious.

Understood from a communicative standpoint, a stimulus may be both a direct message and an encoded message, an expression having both manifest and latent contents and functions. Similarly, the response to such a stimulus often has both manifest and latent meanings, because the receiver has registered, both consciously and also without awareness, the conscious and unconscious meanings of a received message. Thus, a symptomatic or associative response to a stimulus reflects, in part, the unwitting registration of the implications of that stimulus, leading to a responsive encoded message. Quite often, the key factor in sender/receiver exchanges is *unconscious communication* between the participants—expressions whose implications are registered and have led to response outside the awareness of both the sender and the receiver of the encoded messages.

The question arises as to what evidence exists that the receiver has registered the unconscious aspects of a sender's encoded message in some form outside the recipient's awareness. Such evidence is constituted by the receiver's reactions to the imparted message. Typically, they include behaviors and associations that are in keeping with the unconscious implications of the stimulus; in this way there is clear evidence that the stimulus has registered outside of awareness and has led to a responsive communication.

In summary, from a communicative standpoint, a stimulus is an expression that contains both direct and encoded messages. It leads to a response that similarly contains both direct and encoded messages—messages that are *shaped by both the nature of the stimulus and the condition of the receiver*.

In psychotherapy, this latter factor—the condition of the patient/receiver—is mainly the state of his or her inner madness. In addition, however, a receiver's condition is influenced by his or her intrapsychic state, constructive capabilities, genetic history, and the like. In substance, encoded messages lead to important encoded responses. Such reactions thereupon become fresh stimuli leading to still further encoded responses. In this way cycles of unconscious interaction are initiated and carried out. It is the goal of the psychotherapist to develop the techniques to decode such messages, whether they are taking place between a patient and figures in his or her outside life, or, directly, between the patient and therapist within the treatment situation.

From this standpoint, a *symptom* is a dysfunctional encoded response to a stimulus having both manifest and latent meanings. Symptoms usually involve highly disguised encoded messages and are difficult to decode except in a very general way. In contrast, dreams and other kinds of free associations are often the carriers of thinly disguised encoded responses to a stimulus and are more readily decoded. The communicative valence of responses to conscious and unconscious stimuli varies from patient to patient, as does the vehicle of expression. Some behaviors and material are highly meaningful carriers of unconscious expression, whereas others are not. Nevertheless, in the therapeutic situation, *all* of a given patient's associations and behaviors have the *potential* to function as carriers of encoded reactions to the stimuli with which he or she is presently dealing.

Madness itself, then, should be understood as an encoded expression—as unconscious communication, whose underlying meanings and functions, as such, cannot be stated manifestly and directly by the person experiencing that condition. The associations produced in response to the surface forms that madness takes reveals its unconscious basis by way of their derivative aspects. Accordingly, the listening process in psychotherapy must center on efforts to decode the unconscious meanings and functions of madness in light of the stimuli that helped to create its existence.

It should be noted in this regard that a patient's encoded expressions will necessarily reflect his or her registration of unconscious aspects of the therapist's interventions. Patient cure or lack of cure (and even regression) is effected in terms of a therapist's unconscious as well as conscious messages to the patient. One of the goals of psychotherapy is thus to create an interaction wherein the therapist's expressions to the patient are primarily conscious and direct—with the least possible measure of encoded valence (i.e., with as little as possible conveyed to the patient outside the awareness of the therapist). The patient's expressions, on the other hand, should convey far less significant manifest meaning and a far greater proportion of encoded implications.

One must also recognize that although there are countless *potential* unconscious fantasies and perceptions (daydreams and views of others that exist outside of awareness), they are revealed only through encoded expressions and are stated by way of camouflage and transformation. Thus, we can verify the existence only of those fantasies and perceptions that have been activated by immediate stimuli and find expression in a patient's material.

Single- and Multiple-message Communication. The communicative model should reduce the sense of mystery and awe that tends to accompany consideration of unconscious factors in emotional disturbance. It complements and supplements Freud's depth psychology (1900) by placing its emphasis on human expression rather than on human mentation, and by regarding human expression as an adaptive response to stimuli. In communicative terms, primary- and secondary-process thinking can be restated as the human capacity for *single-message* and *multiple-message communication. Single-message communication* is used in response to pragmatic, external issues; in single-message expressions the manifest message is the totality of intended communication. *Multiple-message communication* is used in emotionally charged situations, where irrational factors play a significant role. In multiple-message communication, the manifest expression carries latent meanings, thus permitting an individual to deal simultaneously with both conscious and unconscious aspects of a disturbing stimulus. The mind shifts from one form of expression to the other automatically, as the situation warrants.

As Freud determined, the manifest carrier of a multiple-message is related to its latent implications by a thematic bridge. The communicative approach emphasizes the fact that access to the unconscious meaning of a multi-message behavioral or verbal-affective surface expression is *by way of that surface expression*: The manifest is a sign or symbol of the latent (the signified or symbolized). The theme located in the manifest image or context is derived from and belongs with an image or context that is still unconscious. This is how unconscious communication takes place. Simply stated, one communicates consciously about situation (context) A, while communicating outside of awareness about situation (context) B.

This process, called displacement, is defensive. It protects an individual not only from repressed fantasies and memories, as Freud determined via dreams, but also from threatening perceptions of external situations. Ironically, the means by which we preserve our mental integrity, unconscious communication, when overused, provides the basis for one form of madness—reacting to situation B as though it actually were situation A.

Technical Consequences of the Communicative Model

Because the communicative model dictates a psychology of disguise and transformation, it also dictates a different technique from the one used by the probing depth psychologist. The depth psychologist would describe the ideal therapeutic session as one that resulted in the supposed breakthrough of repressed or unconscious material from the unconscious part of the mind. Phenomenologically, this would be said to occur when, under the patient's own inner pressure or pressure from the therapist, a memory, thought, or fantasy that had not previously been reported emerges in the patient's material. What this generally means, in practical terms, is that the patient has verbalized an implication of an image or thought that he or she had previously reported; at times, however, the new material is indeed distinctive.

The flaw in this line of thought is the belief that unconscious messages can be expressed without disguise or emerge whole cloth into consciousness. This would imply that they had existed as fully-formed secondary-process productions awaiting liberation from the unconscious depths. This is a contradiction in terms.

From the vantage point of the communicative model, an unconscious message reaches conscious expression by way of themes that it shares in common with material already conscious. The patient will unconsciously and quite spontaneously gravitate toward conscious expressions—narratives, dreams, memories—that can encode elements of the total underlying communication. In the ideal communicative-model session, therefore, the patient shifts from one story to another—now to a dream, now to a narrative, next to a memory—spelling out in scattered form a complete encoded message that requires both decoding and synthesis by the therapist. One might say that an unconscious message is something like a nonlinear rebus.

It follows from this postulate that stopping a patient in order to probe a particular image would *disrupt* the flow of communicative expression. The communicative technique relies mainly on silent holding and on the amply confirmed observation that patients will unconsciously and spontaneously shift from one carrier of an encoded message to another until the total underlying communication has been expressed. The psychology of disguise, then, uses silent holding as its primary tool, because it relies on the patient's own need to express his or herself. This strategy is in strong contrast to the direct inquiry more characteristic of the depth psychotherapist until now.

In practical terms, then, when a patient goes from subject to subject, the depth psychotherapist sees resistance, believing that the individual should dig deeper into a particular image or topic. In contrast, the communicative therapist finds that full meaning (low resistance) is most likely when a patient does indeed go from one theme to another, and that concentration on a single area or topic is generally characterized by a relative absence of unconscious implications.

These distinctions have been introduced to indicate some of the unique attributes of the communicative approach, as well as to indicate its fundamental roots in classical psychoanalysis—depth psychology. A thorough discussion requires a consideration of the decoding process attempted from each vantage point and a consideration of other, related issues. I therefore return to the subject later in this book after considering the issues more fully.

SOME BASIC DEFINITIONS

Certain terms introduced in the preceding discussion are particularly relevant to the decoding exercises that constitute the main substance of this workbook. The brief definitions provided here are also designed to summarize the assumptions dictating the communicative approach to patient expression.

1. *Manifest content.* The surface aspect of the patient's associations—their direct, immediate, and self-evident meanings. Surface contents always have meaning per se, but they may (or may not), in addition, contain meanings and implications extending beyond those that are open and direct.

2. *Latent content.* Meaning that is not self-evident in the surface contents of a message (such as a patient's free associations), but is

contained as a disguised or encoded theme within the manifest expression. Latent contents are usually outside the awareness of the sender of the message, whether patient or therapist. On the other hand, the presence of latent contents is in some way signaled or represented in disguised form within the manifest communication.

3. *Derivative*. The term coined by Freud (1900, 1908) to indicate a manifest content that simultaneously expresses a disguised latent meaning. The term is used to imply that the manifest content is derived from the latent raw (dangerous) image. It is to be stressed again that not all manifest free associations function as derivatives.

4. *Encoded message*. This term may be used interchangeably with the term derivative. The term *encoded* (or *transformed*) *message* emphasizes the manifest content as a communicative expression that contains in some disguised or camouflaged form another latent or hidden communication.

5. *Unconscious communication*. A form of expression that takes place outside the awareness of the sender and, sometimes, of the receiver. The primary vehicle of unconscious communication is encoded messages—disguised expressions that contain within their confines displaced and symbolized meanings. In substance, then, unconscious communication occurs by way of disguised messages, usually in the form of narratives and images.

6. *Decoded derivative*. The result of a decoding process wherein the manifest element is treated as a transformed or transposed expression of an underlying message, and the mechanisms of disguise are undone.

PROBLEMS IN DECODING DERIVATIVES

Many therapists approach the study of unconscious communication with dread and awe; many others avoid it entirely. The issues involved are not entirely cognitive, and we may conclude this introductory chapter with a brief perspective on some of the main reasons therapists have difficulty in working with and decoding derivative expressions.

1. First, human beings generally prefer to work with that which is self-evident, directly on the surface, and relatively easy to manipulate. As a result, many therapists are drawn to the surface of their patients' material and attempt to deal with this single level of expression. More complex mental operations are thereby eschewed.

2. Another human tendency is to treat the indirect—anything that cannot be seen directly, touched, immediately understood, and readily manipulated—as though it were nonexistent. The idea that

surface material contains latent meanings, implications not immediately discernible, is alien to many therapists. Therapists may also be hampered in accepting this idea because they understand it to mean that the latent content is mysterious and hidden, rather than recognizing that it is expressed in disguised form on the surface.

3. Psychotherapists, like most human beings, tend to take the line of least resistance, carrying out those tasks that are easiest to do. Decoding a manifest message in order to determine its latent meanings requires mental work, an effort that a therapist may hope to avoid. Furthermore, becuase some meaning is indeed apparent in a patient's surface material, such a therapist develops a sense that there is no need to engage in the more difficult process of deciphering hidden meanings. This impression is surprisingly common, and it is maintained side by side with the realization that Freud gave us a technique for such decoding nearly 100 years ago in *The Interpretation of Dreams* (1900).

4. Highly charged emotional factors also contribute to the therapist's avoidance of the direct translation and recognition of latent meanings (unconscious communications) in a patient's material. With reference to Freud's (1926) basic model, meaningful access to unconscious expressions is experienced as a *danger situation*—an anxiety-provoking endeavor. This is so primarily because encoded messages provide both the therapist and patient with access to the subjective experience and meanings of madness, its determinants and implications. Such realizations are extremely disturbing for both participants to treatment. A truly affective and meaningful experience of patient-madness may occur in both parties to therapy through the impact of realizations related to the patient's encoded messages. The therapist who confines him or herself to attending to manifest contents avoids—and helps the patient to avoid—the highly disturbing implications of the latent messages so contained. In general, although unconscious communication may open avenues to creativity and self-enhancement, it is also far more threatening than most conscious expressions.

5. Communicative studies indicate that a patient's derivative associations often contain highly incisive and compelling encoded perceptions of the therapist's errors, personal difficulties, and other failings—as well as encoded perceptions of his or her assets and constructive attributes when they are present. A decoding of the patient's derivative material, then, often confronts the therapist with highly precise encoded perceptions of his or her own madness. In order to defend themselves against realization of such madness, therapists have preferred to remain fixed on a manifest-content level.

6. Finally, therapists have avoided the decoding of their patients' communications because they would rather not decode the latent

messages in their own interventions. Although some therapists do indeed examine their comments to and behaviors with their patients for implications beyond their intended meanings and the surface contents of their interventions, most therapists attempt neither to examine their own work for encoded messages, nor to decode the disguised messages contained therein. Thus, the defensive adherence by most therapists to the manifest contents of their own interventions has led to the use of a similar defense in attending only to the manifest meanings of their patients' associations.

Psychotherapy attempts to be the insightful resolution of patient-madness. It is constituted by a dyadic relationship and interaction in which madness is the domain, and unconscious communication is the most critical level of expression. Virtually everything that touches upon the therapeutic experience, properly carried out or disturbed, will be influenced by the sanity and madness of the two participants to treatment. No issue in psychotherapy is entirely cognitive or entirely emotional. There is a constant interplay between efforts to learn and apply the techniques of psychoanalytic psychotherapy and the emotional assets and liabilities of the two participants to treatment.

These principles apply quite well to the study of unconscious communication. Although the focus here will be on the cognitive and intellectual issues, and on the development of the required techniques, each therapist must remain mindful of the influence of his or her madness on this learning process and its application. Properly forewarned, let us now move on.

Notes

2 How and Why Messages Are Encoded

DANGER AND DEFENSE

Freud's (1926) basic model of symptom formation (see also Arlow, 1963) provides an excellent and relatively simple model for understanding why individuals automatically and unconsciously encode certain types of messages. This model, elaborated in terms of present-day communicative understanding, proposes that in addition to internal factors, madness is caused by trauma or *danger situations*. In substance, a danger situation is constituted by the apprehension of images and experiences that are highy charged and emotionally threatening to the individual; these may be termed *raw images*. Such experiences lead to an *anxiety response* in the person so confronted, usually in the form of signal anxiety (unless the individual is essentially overwhelmed by the trauma). Other signal affects may also be called into play.

Once the anxiety is sensed or directly experienced, the individual—more precisely his or her ego—mobilizes a series of adaptive responses designed to cope with and/or eliminate the danger situation. Prominent among these responses are intrapsychic and interpersonal defenses. The former are more notable when the danger situation is internal, such as the generation of forbidden instinctual-drive wishes. The latter defenses are mobilized in interpersonal relationships. In most situations, however, the danger situation is complex—a combination of both internal and external factors. In addition, the individual's internal set (pathology and other inner elements) partially determines the manner in which an external danger situation is experienced. On the whole, then, a danger situation is the result of two basic factors: the nature of an external stimulus (unconscious perception) and the manner in which it is interpreted by a given person, which precipitates internal threats from unconscious memories and fantasies.

In terms of the communicative approach, anxiety-producing mental contents may be kept out of consciousness (1) by totally obliterating them from any measure whatsoever of representation or active expression; but failing obliteration, they will (2) emerge disguised (expressed, but remaining unconscious) by way of some communicative vehicle—symptom, affect, thought, fantasy, behavior, and the like—in encoded form. These two forms of defense have certain parallels with the two levels of defensive operation postulated by Freud (1900) in terms of his early topographic model: the one between the systems UCS and PCS, the other between the systems PCS and CS.

Obliteration, or Barrier Repression

A potential unconscious constellation may be totally obliterated because of a combination of two factors: externally, the absence of a stimulus that mobilizes the particular unconscious constellation and, internally, the presence of what may be termed *barrier repression*, a massive defense that permits no derivative leakage or emergence of encoded expression. This description may be viewed as a recasting of what Freud (1915) termed *primal repression*. The defense is also a form of denial, in that potential internal perceptions are entirely obliterated and rendered functionally nonexistent.

Compromise Formations, or Derivative Repression

Potential unconscious expressions that are not obliterated by barrier repression, by definition, find access to conscious communication. In classic psychoanalytic terms, if the defenses mobilized by the signal of anxiety in response to a danger situation are adequate, anxiety diminishes, and the situation is resolved in adaptive fashion. If, however, for some reason these defenses fail (either because of the intensity of the danger or impairments of the ego's defenses), a compromise response to the danger situation will take place.

In other words, when repressed material gains access to conscious communication, it always does so by way of a compromise between open expression of the raw unconscious image and the need to disguise—remain unconscious of—the underlying image, that is, to defend against it. This situation represents a form of porous or what is called *derivative repression*, wherein the underlying raw image (perception and/or fantasy or memory) remains unconscious and outside of the individual's awareness, while gaining access to conscious awareness in some disguised form. The term *disguise* here thus indicates that a theme belonging to a raw unconscious image has been displaced onto a conscious situation, thereby creating a symbol of what remains out of awareness in its true form. This is the primary means by which the human mind encodes threatening, dangerous, anxiety-provoking raw images.

To clarify, in communicative terms, *barrier repression* implies noncommunication and the destruction of meaning; the raw image is kept completely out of awareness, obliterated. *Derivative repression* implies the presence of encoded meaning. Displacement and symbolization (representation of one thing by another) are the two mechanisms by means of which derivative repression operates.

The compromise formations that we call *symptoms* are not only the products of intrapsychic (and interactional-interpersonal) defenses; they are also, in this view, forms of encoded, disguised communication. In a compromise response, all aspects of the danger situation—the external stimulus, the internal dangers that have been aroused by the stimulus (usually in the form of instinctual-drive expressions), and the somewhat inadequate defenses used by the individual to protect him or herself from the components of the danger situation—will find some means of expression and representation. Such a compromise response, therefore, expresses both the danger situation and the defenses designed to cope with it in disguised form.

An emotional symptom such as a phobia is a classic example of this type of compromise formation. In the fear of heights, for example, the external danger situation may involve high places and the fear of jumping or falling to one's death. The internal danger situation aroused by that experience may involve an impulsive sexual or aggessive wish. Signal anxiety is thus called into play in anticipation of a confrontation with the danger situation itself. The result may be avoidance of heights or the use of a variety of intrapsychic defenses that permit access to heights without emotional collapse.

Upon analysis, the fear of heights may be found, for example, to represent the fear of an erection vis-a-vis a boy's incestuous wish to copulate with his mother. In that case, one would conclude that the anxiety involved has prompted the use of the intrapsychic defenses of displacement and symbolization (the basic communicative defenses as well), thereby enabling the boy to continue to relate to his mother and to treat an external/internal danger situation connected with that relationship as a danger located elsewhere.

In this example, we can see how the very defenses that protect the child from anxiety also create the situation of madness. Emotional dysfunctions are irrational and are not based on the reality of the immediate situation. It is indeed symptomatic to fear heights, and the fear can be managed easily with proper controls. It is well to note, however, that it is also appropriate to be anxious and fearful of wishes to have intercourse with one's own mother. Were the child simply to fear such a wish, no madness would be in evidence.

To restate the basis of this process in communicative terms, a danger situation is constituted by a series of raw images with threatening internal and external implications. These raw images involve both dangerous perceptions and highly charged fantasies. The ego tends to act unconsciously and with great rapidity in response to such situations, mobilizing the signal of anxiety that creates an almost immediate defensive response. Because of this, the danger situation itself—the raw images—do not register consciously, but instead are registered outside of awareness. The conscious experience is therefore a product of compromise, a cross between the raw image and the defensive disguises that render that image unrecognizable. In the clinical situation, there would be evidence of that compromise formation—a conscious association or image that contains some representation of the threatening raw image as well as an important measure of defensive disguise. As can be seen, then, such a manifest association, constituted as a derivative of an underlying raw image, renders the communicative representation of the danger situation in disguised form—offering it portrayal and expression, though not in full and direct force and form.

Transformed manifest associations prevent the experience of anxiety, because they sufficiently disguise the nature of the raw image or danger situation. Nonetheless, the danger situation has in fact found representation in an altered and encoded form. It follows that a proper effort at decoding will reveal both the nature of the dangerous stimulus that has been subjected to disguise as well as any and all defenses and other adaptive responses to this threat.

It should be stressed in this regard that dangerous raw images which have been represented in disguised form involve not only unconscious fantasy and memory formations. Equally threatening are perceptions of others that must be represented and yet disguised in order to maintain an ongoing relationship but also to cope with the danger involved. In this type of situation, it is a perception of someone that remains unconscious as the potential raw image. Communicative studies have shown unconscious perceptions to play a highly significant role in the access of unconscious fantasies and memories to disguised representation. As such, they are a factor in unconscious communication and in neurosis-formation (the development of madness) which has been greatly underestimated by psychotherapists, especially as it applies to the ongoing therapeutic interaction. This is why I am using the term *raw images*; it is an inclusive term that can incorporate dangerous perceptions as well as threatening fantasies and memories.

Lie-Barrier Formations

It is important to realize that when an individual is using a repression-barrier defense, thereby obliterating a raw image, an observer would lack any evidence for the unconscious registration of the image and/or an encoded response. In the clinical situation, the existence of this type of barrier defense is established by recognizing the activation of a traumatic stimulus for the patient's communicative responses, and then observing the virtual absence of derivative reactions in the patient's material. In the place of such encoded expressions, there are flat associations, whose meanings appear to be restricted to manifest contents.

Such material is entirely unrelated to and disconnected from the postulated emotional, psychological, and communicative disturbance that is being sealed off. In terms established by Bion (1977), the patient's material at such junctures involves conscious statements that serve merely as barriers to underlying chaos. Thus, the patient substitutes functionally irrelevant or meaningless material for the highly meaningful and relevant encoded responses that are being obliterated. These manifest contents are therefore segments of fiction vis-a-vis the true inner disturbance of the patient. In terms of the interactional and psychodynamic emotional truths of the moment, the surface material constitutes both a destruction of these truths and the substitution of lies—the use of lie-barrier formations.

The most important implication of this discussion for the moment is the realization, then, that the patient's manifest associations may be either highly meaningful with respect to unconscious communication or quite devoid of such meaning. In the psychotherapist's quest for meaning in a patient's material, the unconscious need and communicative capability of such patients to destroy meaningful expression has, in general, been overlooked. Given the existence of an intrapsychic and/or interpersonal conflict, and a related symptom of madness, the first issue in any psychotherapy or psychoanalytic session is to establish whether or not the patient is meaningfully communicating the unconscious factors in such a disturbance and, moreover, to establish just how clear and usable (interpretable) the patient's expressions are. Before issues of dynamics, genetics, narcissism, and the like can be considered, problems of communication must be taken into account. This is one of the basic contentions of the communicative approach and a fundamental tenet out of which the present volume has been created.

DANGER SITUATIONS AND DISGUISE: EXERCISE 2.1

The material for this brief exercise is taken from the final session with a 45-year-old woman who was seen in once-weekly psychotherapy for episodes of depression. She begins this last hour as follows.

> *Patient*: One of the boys in the class that I teach at religious school is leaving town. I don't know if I will ever see him again. I wanted to hug him goodbye. My son is leaving for an out-of-town college. I thought of the time my father left us when I was a child. Yesterday, at religious school, I thought of having an affair with the principal.
>
> In the space provided below, answer the following questions:

1. What is the main external danger situation for the patient in this excerpt? (Notice the overall theme or themes in the patient's association. Is there a situation that we know about in the

therapeutic interaction which the patient does not mention directly, but involves a theme or themes in common with the situations that are mentioned?)

2. Identify the patient's encoded representations (portrayals) of the danger situation. How do they indicate the patient's use of communicative defense and disguise? What are the specific mechanisms used by the patient for this purpose?

3. The encoded messages are not only alluding to the external danger situation. They indicate that the patient is attempting to cope with the danger situation. What wishes have been mobilized by these attempts, thereby creating an internal danger situation as well?

4. What conscious memory is the danger situation evoking?

5. Can you detect at least three encoded or unconscious fantasies (and/or memories) that the danger situation has also evoked? State each fantasy wish as a decoded (raw) image.

Answers:

1. The main danger situation for the patient is the termination of her psychotherapy.

2. The patient has largely made use of displacement and symbolization in her allusions to the external danger situation. Rather than alluding directly to the therapist's abandonment (a major meaning for the patient of the termination experience), the patient mentions the loss of a boy in her class, of her son, and of her father in childhood. There is, therefore, displacement away from the therapist and therapeutic relationship onto each of these three individuals and life-situations. Each involves an aspect of loss and termination, and therefore some measure of symbolization—that is, each expresses in some disguised form a meaning of the ending of the patient's psychotherapy. Each allusion represents a compromise formation that expresses the theme of separation and loss, without

referring directly to termination with the therapist. Each of the portrayals describes the danger situation—termination—in a form that is disguised and yet discernible to the sensitive decoder. Furthermore, each of these representations simultaneously expresses a particular meaning, present and genetic, of the danger situation for the patient.

The encoded portrayals of danger situations that are constituted by interventions by the therapist (i.e., stimuli of importance in the therapeutic context with which the patient is attempting to cope) are of particular significance in psychotherapy, because the patient's most meaningful unconscious communications involve encoded reactions to the interventions of the therapist. Thus, in offering an interpretation to the patient, it becomes essential to do so in light of the patient's own material and representations.

3. As for the patient's efforts to cope with the danger situation, termination, we may first recognize the adaptive efforts reflected in her initial associations. Here, through a series of encoded messages, the patient attempts to express her perceptions of the situation and her responses to its main meanings for her. More specifically, through the use of displacement, the patient states, first, that she wanted to hug the boy who was leaving her class. It may be hypothesized that the patient entertains a similar wish toward the therapist. This internal wish, connected to sexual instinctual drives, constitutes a fresh danger situation. It stimulates the use of disguise so that the patient's manifest wish is directed toward a child in her class (where the wish is relatively appropriate), rather than toward the therapist (where the wish would be inappropriate). In this way, we observe how an external danger situation may create a responsive internal danger.

In a similar fashion, the patient's thought of having an affair with the principal of the school, linked in associational sequence to the representations of termination, may be seen to represent a disguised and displaced sexual wish directed toward the therapist. This, too, is an internal danger situation created by the external trauma of termination. Once again, the disguise permits open expression of a wish directed toward someone with whom the patient is comfortable in entertaining the fantasy of an affair. This permits an expression of the wish without directly connecting it to the therapist, with whom the wish would be experienced as anxiety-provoking, dangerous, and forbidden.

4. The danger situation of termination has led to the patient's conscious recall of a time when her father left the family. This is not an *unconscious* memory, but a conscious association.

5. The danger situation of termination appears to have evoked several unconscious fantasies within the patient. First, there is the wish to hug the therapist, expressed manifestly in a different

relationship, but clearly a reaction to the loss of the therapist. Here, the dangerous raw image can be stated as follows: I wish to hug you when I leave. Addressed to the therapist, this would be anxiety-provoking and leads to communicative defense.

A second unconscious fantasy memory would in some way link the therapist with the patient's father. The dangerous raw image may be to the following effect: You are deserting me as my father deserted me in the past. This particular connection seems threatening to the patient, who therefore displaces her feelings about the current situation with the therapist onto the remembered situation with the father, thereby utilizing a simple associational element to express the underlying raw image or thought.

Finally, the most dangerous or anxiety-provoking raw image may be stated as follows: You (the therapist) are leaving me, and I wish to hold onto you by having an affair with you. This is an evoked unconscious fantasy that finds expression in displaced form, in connection with the principal rather than with the therapist.

Through this brief exercise, we have seen how external and internal danger situations are subjected to communicative disguise. Similar disguises are applied to evoked memories and fantasies. It is raw images of this kind that lead to unconscious and automatic encoding by patients in psychotherapy.

MECHANISMS OF DISGUISE

As I indicated earlier, Freud was interested in the means by which an anxiety-provoking latent thought was transformed into a manifest communicative element. His findings (1900) appear to be as valid and useful today as they were at the time of their development. The four mechanisms of transformation that must be undone or reversed in order to decode disguised material are: displacement, symbolization, condensation, and secondary-revision. We have already been dealing with the first two. In this section each is presented in light of the foregoing exercise.

Displacement, or Transposition

Displacement always implies a shift of target by which a raw unconscious message is portrayed by a different and conscious vehicle. It is important to realize that displacement occurs automatically and unconsciously. Furthermore, the selection of the displaced target is based upon some measure of similarity between the raw message and the vehicle onto which it is displaced. Thus, there will always be a theme or meaning that is shared by the original raw message and its conscious vehicle.

In substance, then, when an individual wishes to encode a message, he or she will shift the sphere of communication from A to B—from one topic to another, from one person to a second person, and so forth. Entirely outside of awareness, while speaking or imagining in the area of B, the underlying and raw images concern A. Through displacement, human beings work over many emotionally charged images and issues in terms of surface preoccupations that express and yet conceal the underlying problems.

Displacement was utilized by the woman patient in the foregoing excerpt. The latent raw image concerned the therapist's decision to terminate her psychotherapy and the fact that she was engaged in her final session. Instead of talking directly about the termination experience, however, quite unconsciously the patient chose to displace these concerns—her perceptions and reactions—onto other spheres of reference. The result was the allusion to the boy who was leaving her class, the reference to her son leaving home, and the memory of her father's abandonment of the family. Given that the central stimulus and raw image involved the therapist and the termination of the patient's treatment, each of these images can be seen as displaced from the treatment relationship onto another sphere that shares a common theme with the first—separation and loss. Individuals unconsciously seek out experiences suitable for displacement to serve as vehicles for this type of unconscious expression. Through displacement, there can be considerable unconscious working over the important emotional issues.

Unconscious communication, then, is essentially communication through displacement. In general, displaced images tend to be rich in nuance and meaning, whereas direct messages tend to be far more linear and pragmatic. In psychotherapy, it has been found empirically that when a patient works over a particular trauma on a manifest level, there is little genuine insight, especially into unconscious factors. In contrast, when a patient works over the same issue through displacement, the yield of meaning, and especially of unconscious meaning, proves to be considerable. Thus, displacement is an extremely adaptive means through which human beings work over highly charged emotional difficulties.

As is true of every psychic mechanism, however, displacement may be used pathologically and maladaptively. In order to be useful to the individual, the displaced working over must eventually be applied consciously to the traumatic situation—that is, directly to the raw image that is causing the disturbance. Although the exact effects of unconsciously working over a displaced disturbance are not entirely clear, it appears that communicative adaptation on this level does not itself lead to conscious insight and direct adaptation. There must be an ultimate moment of insight whereby the displaced efforts reach conscious realization as such. Following insight, direct integration proves feasible and behavioral adaptation is fostered.

When displacement is overused or leads to unconscious behavioral responses (as though situation A were actually situation B), it shifts from serving as a mechanism of defensive protection to being a cause of emotional disturbance. For example, if the woman in the foregoing excerpt were to react to the departure of her son or the student in her class based on fantasies and images that pertain unconsciously to the therapist, her behaviors might be quite out of keeping with the realities of the mother/son relationship or of the classroom situation. Displacement can thus lead to manifest behaviors that constitute forms of madness and is a factor in the creation of psychopathology. Again, the very psychic defenses that protect the individual from madness can paradoxically become the cause of madness itself.

Symbolization, or Transformation and Representation

The second fundamental means by which human beings encode raw messages is to portray the underlying image with a different but thematically related image. Here, the term *symbolism* is utilized in its broadest sense to imply the representation or portrayal of a raw image by a different though related image. In simple terms, one thing is conveyed by another.

In a later portion of the session excerpted in the exercise, the patient said that she was worried about losing her job. Here, the patient is symbolizing (or representing) the raw image involving the loss of the therapist by concerns over losing her job. The job situation can be understood thus to represent the treatment situation. This substitution permits the patient to impersonalize her loss.

Returning for a moment to the three displaced images that the patient used to portray the loss of the therapist in the excerpt proper, one will notice that the measure of symbolization being employed is minimal. Both the boy leaving the patient's class and the departure of the patient's son simply portray or represent the loss of the therapist; there is no other notable measure of symbolization. The same principle applies to the patient's conscious memory of the loss of her father. Of course, there are complex interconnections between the therapist and the patient's son and father in particular, but these will not be considered here. They simply hint at the layers of meaning that can be inherent in the use of displacement and symbolization, and to the patient's particular choice of a displacement figure and symbol.

Still later in the same session, the patient spoke of a co-worker who had lost part of her finger in childhood. Here, the patient unconsciously speaks of losing the therapist by consciously talking about the loss of a bodily part. The latter is being used as a symbol of the former. As can be seen, displacement is an inherent aspect of symbolization, although symbolization need not be used when displacement is applied. Further, it is evident that the *choice of symbol* is fraught with unconscious meaning: Losing a job has far different implications than losing a body part, so that the choice of one or the other to portray the loss of a therapist is significant. In decoding a symbol, then, attention must be paid not only to the underlying raw message, but also to the unconscious selection of the representational vehicle.

Displacement and symbolization are the two basic means of human encoding, or transformation. There are, however, certain additional mechanisms that are applied to render a surface encoded message meaningful in and of itself, while simultaneously portraying a rather different embedded raw image or communication. Each of these mechanisms was described by Freud (1900) in his delineation of primary-process functioning.

Condensation

When an individual communicates by way of encoded messages, using disguised derivatives, a single message will often contain two or more encoded expressions. For evident reasons of mental economy, several raw and emotionally charged messages will be conveyed in a single manifest allusion. Condensation is most easily recognized when a decoder is aware of two or more significant, traumatic triggers or stimuli for a given surface communication. An examination of the manifest derivative message in light of the implications of each trigger renders feasible a separate decoding of the single surface message in terms of each stimulus; each of these efforts reveal a different underlying raw message. The human mind quite unconsciously selects as a manifest representational vehicle an image that shares in common the multiple themes contained in the several raw images condensed in the surface expression.

To illustrate, we may return again to the aforementioned patient. Her surface image involving concerns about losing her job condenses her reactions to the raw and traumatic images (triggers or stimuli) that pertain both to the loss of her psychotherapist and to the loss of her son. The same image apparently contains as well an effort to rework the earlier childhood trauma of the temporary loss of her father. In similar fashion, the allusion to the loss of the finger condenses portrayals of each of the present and past losses with which the patient is concerned.

Secondary Revision and Concern for Representability

There is a final unconscious operation carried out by the ego in dealing with encoded images. A raw but threatening image is first transformed into a disguised manifest element with which it shares a common theme. When unconscious communication is mobilized, such as in the course of free association or in a dream, the ego encodes a series of raw images or deals with a single raw image by way of manifest derivatives that convey a number of implications of the underlying threatening image. However, the ego's need for logical and rational surface messages—that is, to not appear mad at the level of direct communication—leads to an intolerance of manifestly fragmented communications. Instead, there is an unconscious quest for sensibility and integration. Overall, there is a fundamental need to produce a surface message that makes sense, that tells a reasonable story, or contains a logical narrative. For this reason, each sequence of manifest derivative elements is subjected to some measure of what Freud called secondary revision in order to produce a sensible surface communication. During this process, the form this communication will take—whether a sequence of thoughts, affects, and free association or a series of images in a dream—is also taken into account.

One might picture an ego function of unconsciously casting about for an experience, memory, story, or dream that will serve as a manifest and derivative vehicle for a sequence of unconscious messages that the individual wishes to convey for reasons of adaptation. Once these vehicles have been unconsciously selected, the manner in which the person further selects particular elements from these incidents or stories and shapes the means by which they are reported will tell a sensitive listener a great deal about how the unconscious raw images are being experienced. In this way, through a series of second-order operations, the individual is able to unconsciously communicate a highly selective manifest narrative which simultaneously contains one or more critical raw images and their implications.

In the foregoing clinical vignette, the patient communicated a series of logically connected, rational thoughts and feelings—images. This sequence of derivative expressions also served to represent disturbing stimuli (latent raw images) with which the patient was dealing. These manifest representations were nevertheless *selected*; the manner in which they were selected and reported enabled the patient to communicate *specific* encoded meanings that are important to her as an individual. In other words, the human mind has the capacity to automatically and unconsciously convey a series of manifest images, each logically consistent and part of an integrated surface whole, but simultaneously conveying a series of extremely meaningful, if fragmented, emotionally pertinent encoded raw images.

ENCODED COMMUNICATION: EXERCISE 2.2

The following material is excerpted from a psychotherapy session of a young, depressed, married man with problems in impulse control. He was being seen once a week by a woman therapist. The therapist had unwittingly extended the patient's previous session by some ten minutes. At the beginning of this hour, the patient gave the therapist a gift: a book on the excessive use of psychotropic medications. Once seated in his chair, the patient spoke as follows:

> *Patient*: I've been taking my medication for my depression, but I'm afraid that I'm addicted to drugs. I always go too far. I don't know how to set limits for my children. I had this dream of a strange woman touching me sexually, holding on to me, and not letting me go. I gave my son too much money for his birthday.

Attempt to answer the following questions based on the foregoing clinical material:

1. What are the main stimuli for these manifest associations?

2. Is there evidence for the use of displacement? Identify those images that appear to be displaced.

3. Is there evidence for the use of symbolization and encoded representation? Attempt to identify those manifest elements that contain encoded portrayals of the main stimuli for these associations—the therapist's two interventions (extending the hour and accepting the book). What are the implications of the symbols selected by the patient to express his encoded perceptions of the therapist and his reactive fantasies?

4. Identify those images that condense representations of, and reactions to, each of these major stimuli.

Answers:

1. The main stimuli for the patient's associations reside in the therapist's two interventions: (1) her ten-minute extension of the patient's previous session, and (2) her acceptance of the patient's gift—the book on psychotropic medications. These are both highly threatening interventions, creating anxiety-provoking images (perceptions, and possible evoked fantasies) for the patient. Though gratifying, the implications of these interventions constitute danger situations that will lead to the mobilization of communicative defense in the form of displacement and disguise (symbolization). It is for this reason that we should seek encoded latent meanings to these manifest associations. These disguised meanings derive from two sources: (1) the nature and implications of the stimuli and (2) the patient's own inner propensities, especially the nature of the patient's psychopathology.

2. Because the main stimuli for these associations and their unconscious implications reside in the interventions of the therapist, any association that does not allude directly to the two interventions at hand (and at the very least, to the therapist herself) are considered to be displaced *from* the therapist *to* other figures. Thus, the patient's allusion to his addictive state is displaced from the therapist onto himself, in that the therapist's extension of the patient's hour and acceptance of a gift both have dangerously addictive (pathologically incorporative) attributes. In similar fashion, the patient's self-image that he always goes too far is displaced from the therapist onto himself and contains another encoded attribute of both interventions. Still further, in the patient's comment regarding his inability to set limits for his children, there lies another displaced image of the therapist ascribed to himself. This is an encoded

perception of (1) the therapist's failure to end the session on time (a temporal limit), and (2) her acceptance of the gift (the failure to set an interpersonal limit or boundary).

It is extremely common for patients to displace images of their therapists onto themselves. This form of disguise often goes unrecognized by the therapist, who reacts by defending against hurtful encoded perceptions of the implications of his or her erroneous interventions. The evidence that such displacement is in operation is obtained by identifying the intervention to which the patient is responding, recognizing its many implications, and then discovering a representation of one of these meanings as it is attributed to a person other than the therapist and to a situation other than the psychotherapy. Virtually every important encoded image in psychotherapy involves a displaced perception—and more rarely, fantasy—of the therapist onto another individual.

The next displacement in this excerpt is from the therapist to the "strange woman" in the dream who is touching the patient (a displaced image of a meaning of the therapist's acceptance of the book) and who attempts to hold onto him sexually (an unconscious implication of both of these errant interventions). Associations later in the session indicated that the dream was dreamt in anticipation that the therapist would indeed accept this gift, as she had done with other small gifts in the past.

Finally, the patient displaces onto himself a perception of the therapist (in light of her interventions) by shifting the arena from therapist/patient to patient/son in the allusion of his giving the boy too much money for his birthday.

In all, then, each of the images in this session is displaced from the therapist onto some other figure, mainly the patient himself. If the patient had alluded directly to the therapist's acceptance of the book or to the extension of the hour, the images of the therapist would have been expressed on a manifest content level, hence precipitating no displacement.

3. In considering the use of symbols, in the following answers I identify specific rather than general portrayals as they appear sequentially in the material, commenting briefly on the implications derived from the selection of each symbol.

a. The medication to which the patient is addicted may be seen to represent, first, the gift that the therapist accepted and, second, the extension of the patient's hour. Here, the medication, as a tranquilizing substance, is used to portray the book; the patient is indicating that he perceives the book to have similar utility for the therapist—that is, she has accepted the gift in order to diminish her level of anxiety. The medication also implies oral incorporation, another unconscious implication of accepting the book. In general, the selection of a symbol is based, first, on consensually validated implications of the intervention of the therapist, and second, on the pathology of the patient, which influences the particular form that the portrayal takes. This latter factor is an important determinant of the specific meaning (among many) of the intervention to which the patient unconsciously chooses to respond.

Next the image of addiction symbolizes the extension of an hour as an incorporative swallowing up of, or clinging to, the patient. Here, the symbol is not especially definitive, but there is clear shared meaning between the manifest image (seeing the patient beyond the end of his session) and the symbol by which it is portrayed (being addicted to a substance, and therefore needing it too much). In this way, we are identifying the theme that bridges the manifest and latent content and permits the use of a particular manifest image as a means of conveying a specific latent perception.

b. The manifest image of going too far is somewhat indefinite, but serves to portray both the acceptance of a gift (which extends the appropriate boundaries of the therapeutic relationship) and more clearly, the extension of the patient's hour—going too far timewise in the psychotherapy. In this latter instance, displacement seems to carry out almost all of the camouflage work, because the image is directly descriptive of a perceived intervention.

c. The manifest image of the patient not knowing how to set limits for his children again portrays the therapist's failure to maintain appropriate interpersonal boundaries, as reflected in her acceptance of the gift and in her failure to set limits concerning the extension of the hour.

d. The patient's dream of the woman trying to hold onto him sexually involves the unconscious implication of physical contact inherent in accepting a gift, and the unconscious seductive meanings such acceptance can have for a patient. Similarly, the extension of the patient's hour involves holding onto him in a manner that has unconscious sexual undertones. In this instance, the patient has symbolized an instinctual-drive-related meaning of the two interventions at hand.

e. The patient's giving his son too much money for his birthday uses the money as a symbol for the book—both share the gift theme. In a more remote fashion, the extra money represents the extra time that the therapist gave the patient, also a kind of gift.

In all, both displacement and symbolization were used actively by this patient in response to these two highly threatening interventions and the unconscious image of the therapist experienced as a result.

4. In identifying the nature of the patient's representations, we have moved toward recognizing those images that condense portrayals and reactions to both interventions. The following show the clearest use of condensation—that is, a simultaneous portrayal or reaction to both the therapist's extension of the hour and her acceptance of the gift.

a. Addiction to medication—condenses the addictive qualities of both interventions and their incorporative aspects.

b. Going too far—condenses the lack of boundaries reflected by the therapist in both efforts.

c. Not setting limits—also condenses an important meaning of both interventions.

d. The entrapping and seductive aspects of the dream—condenses qualities of both the gift and the extended hour.

e. Finally, the excessive gift given to the son on his birthday touches upon the gift accepted by the therapist as well as upon the extended hour. This last image is an especially cogent instance of condensation: Giving too much money as a manifest derivative contains encoded within its meanings accepting an inappropriate gift and extending a session beyond its limits. In condensation, *an image with a theme shared by two or more stimuli serves to represent implications of both triggers*. One should note that the decoding of condensed images depends heavily on being able to recognize the two or more triggers that have contributed to the development of the derivative representation (the manifest element that contains within its latent contents implications of both stimuli).

ADDITIONAL FACTORS IN THE ENCODING PROCESS

Good and Poor Vehicles for Encoded Messages

Patients in psychotherapy utilize a wide variety of communicative vehicles—dreams, visual and auditory images, memories, narratives, allusions to shows and plays, affects, symptoms, and such. Although any of these message carriers may contain encoded meanings discernible in light of a particular stimulus, certain message forms are especially likely to function as meaningful derivatives—manifest carriers of latent messages. Among these, narratives and images are especially prominent, including all types of dream reports, early recollections, the details of recent events, allusions to creative works, and the like. Unconscious communication is carried out almost entirely by narratives of this kind. Often, each major segment of the tale, and each story in a sequence, will contain one or more specific encoded elements; together, they coalesce into a critical extended unconscious message. In principle, then, a therapist should be alert to the likelihood of derivative communication when a patient is expressing him or herself in one of these ways.

Among the relatively poor carriers of derivative or encoded meaning, the following are most frequently observed: (1) ruminative and repetitive surface material in which the patient repeats the same theme with little variation again and again; (2) manifest allusions to the psychotherapist and to the treatment situation: This type of material is relatively devoid of derivative meaning, because the patient's main motive for encoding messages in psychotherapy is derived from threatening raw images of the psychotherapist; the least likely individual to whom a patient will allude, then, in encoding messages about the therapist is the therapist him or herself (for further details see Langs 1982, in press); (3) intellectualizations, cliches, self-interpretations and other forms of speculation. This last category is not an uncommon form of communication from patients and includes speculations regarding their own hostility, dependency needs, tendency to cling to others, and similar intellectualized or formula considerations that are lacking in image and narrative qualities. At times, psychotherapists will make inferences from such material, believing that they are tapping important unconscious messages. In actual clinical practice, such inferences do not reflect true unconscious encoding and have little or nothing to do with unconscious communication.

In addition to these more common means of single-message, nonderivative expression, a particular narrative or image may actually prove functionally meaningless with respect to unconscious content when the stimulus for the patient's material is known. In such instances, where a decoding process that considers pertinent stimuli from the therapist proves infeasible, it is often possible to engage in isolated symbolic decoding. Because these clinical observations touch on more complicated issues, they are considered again toward the end of this volume.

As a final note, it is important to recognize that both affects and symptoms tend to be poor carriers of derivative meaning. By and large, a symptom does not reveal its own unconscious structure, but instead requires an associational matrix to illuminate its unconscious meanings. In psychotherapy the clinical work often involves the decoding of such ongoing material as a means of determining the actual unconscious basis for the symptomatic expression.

The Encoding of Representations

It is well to distinguish two interrelated and yet different types of symbolization or encoding. The first is fairly straightforward: The representational vehicle encodes a *portrayal* of the raw image itself. The second is more complex in that the representational vehicle encodes *the meanings and implications* of the raw image, rather than its inherent characteristics.

An encoded representation, or portrayal, may be illustrated by the material mentioned earlier in this chapter. If we consider the therapist's acceptance of a gift from the male patient, we may see that the gift-giving itself is represented or portrayed with almost no disguise by another situation involving gift-giving, wherein the patient gave birthday money to his son. Some measure of disguise enters the situation in that money is substituted for the book accepted by the therapist, and the two are tied together through the underlying gift theme. Other possible means by which the same gift may have been portrayed in the patient's associations would include, among others, an allusion to receiving a package from someone, a reference to a teacher who insisted that his ideas be accepted by the class without question (a relatively disguised portrayal), or an allusion to a salary bonus. Because each portrayal involves a selected symbol, it also conveys in disguised form a particular meaning or implication of the raw image. In general, then, a manifest derivative that conveys in some disguised form an image by means of which the actual nature of the raw image itself may be identified is called an encoded representation, or portrayal.

In the psychotherapeutic situation, the recognition of such portrayals is of considerable importance. As indicated, they involve raw images created by threatening and traumatic interventions from the therapist. The unconscious meanings and implications of such inventions will generally occupy the balance of the patient's encoded response. In the treatment hour, the goal, as a rule, is to demonstrate to the patient that on an unconscious level he or she is reacting to a particularly stressful intervention and has experienced it in terms of a variety of encoded meanings. One can accomplish this only if we can point to a clear portrayal on the patient's part of the intervention itself. Ideally, this portrayal will occur manifestly, without disguise and in passing—that is, the patient will mention the intervention directly, without extended comment. But clear encoded portrayals can also be used to indicate to the patient that something related to a particularly important image has gone on in the psychotherapy. The therapist plays back the portrayal with special emphasis, using this particular representation to organize the patient's additional derivatives.

In the case of the patient who gave his therapist a book, such an intervention could begin with a comment about the patient's allusion to his concerns about an excessive gift or a special bonus. As long as there has been some general reference to the therapist or to the psychotherapy, the therapist could then indicate that the concern must involve something that has taken place within the treatment situation. It is in this way that portrayals of underlying and encoded raw images prove highly critical to the intervening process. Furthermore, because of the clinical importance of such portrayals, and the ease with which they may be recognized, it is well to single out this particular form of encoded communication.

The Encoding of Meaning, or Implications

There is a strong tendency within the human mind to automatically and unconsciously sense and detect a wide variety of implications for each traumatic raw message (stimulus) with which one must deal. Thus, patients in psychotherapy are highly sensitive to the implications of interventions from their therapists. Although each class of interventions shares common, universal meanings, patients tend to *selectively encode* meanings that have special relevance to their own lives and conflicts—and especially to their own psychopathology and madness. In order to accurately detect the encoded implications of a patient's raw images, a therapist must draw upon self-knowledge, an understanding of human intrapsychic and interpersonal dynamics and conflicts, knowledge of the patient, and the entire scope of psychoanalytic theory and its insights.

For the moment it will suffice to illustrate some of the more evident implications of the stimuli that we have been considering in this chapter. For example, a therapist's acceptance of a gift from a patient implies physical contact and incorporative neediness—addiction. The patient involved encoded such perceptions in his dream of the woman who touched him sexually and in the allusion to his own addiction to medication. The medication was used to portray the gift in disguised fashion (a fairly heavily encoded portrayal), whereas the comment about addiction involved a simple displacement of one of the meanings of the gift transaction both for the therapist and for the patient. A therapist's acceptance of a gift also implies a failure to establish clear and proper interpersonal boundaries between the patient and therapist and a related failure to set appropriate and necessary limits. Both of those implications were portrayed through displacement in references made by the patient to himself.

PORTRAYALS AND IMPLICATIONS: EXERCISE 2.3

The patient is a young woman in once weekly psychotherapy for severe mood swings and marital difficulties. In one particular session the patient mentioned a consultation that she had arranged for her three-year-old daughter, because of a serious leg injury. The therapist, a woman psychiatrist, knew that the consultant did not treat children and became alarmed about the situation. Toward the end of that hour, she advised the patient to cancel the consultation and to see a pediatric orthopedist. The succeeding session was flat and without derivative material; the associations seemed restricted to single-message communications. The following is a brief extract from the beginning of the next hour:

> *Patient*: I had a dream about you. You insisted on showing me how to pack my van. You were just like my mother, bossing me around. I objected but then did what you asked. In another dream, I was with my daughter (the three-year-old), and a woman on a horse was after us. Then I was in a car, about to have sex with a handsome man, when my sister comes in and kisses him. I was furious she invaded my space. I thought about the affair my sister had with our cousin.

It may be noted as an aside that the patient had recently inadvertently met the therapist's husband.

For this exercise, do the following:

1. Identify the best encoded representations or portrayals of the stimulus that has created the raw and threatening image to which the patient was adapting in this session—the therapist's recommendation of a physician for the patient's daughter.

2. Identify as many of the encoded implications of this intervention as you can detect in this material.

Answers:

It is evident that this patient at first made little use of displacement; in the first dream narrative she alludes directly to the therapist, displacing away from the treatment situation only the setting and the nature of the therapist's directive. The remainder of the material, however, reflects a full use of the displacement process: all of the manifest material touches on individuals other than the therapist and refers to settings different from the treatment situation.

This particular excerpt is constituted by a series of dream reports, and, as can be seen, such imagery can be rich in derivative expression. Reported dreams are usually narrative in form, and therefore potentially strong carriers of encoded meaning. It is evident, too, that there is considerable use of symbolism and representation in this material (see following).

1. Without offering an extended discussion (for supportive background material, see especially Langs, 1982), it may be proposed that the therapist's well-meaning intervention was neither neutral nor interpretive, and, in the main, an inappropriate manipulation of the patient, an invasion of her space, and a violation of her right to autonomy. In a situation of this kind, where a therapist has a legitimate concern for the well-being of a patient or her child, it is often possible to interpret the patient's misguided efforts by using her material in a way that entirely avoids the use of intrusive directives. No matter how well intended, they are consistently

perceived (unconsciously) by patients in a manner not unlike the woman presently under consideration (see answer 2).

The therapist's intervention is the stimulus and raw image to which the patient is reacting and adapting in encoded fashion in this particular hour. The best portrayal of the stimulus itself—the therapist's directive advice—appears in the first dream, where the therapist insists on showing the patient how to pack her van. Although the therapist is alluded to manifestly, displacement is used with respect to the setting and the nature of the directive: There is a shift from the psychotherapy situation to the van, and the directive is changed from medical advice to parking instructions. The theme that links the manifest derivative to its latent portrayal is the therapist's insistence on showing the patient how to do something—something that, by implication, the patient should know how to do on her own. This portrayal is further reinforced by the allusion to the therapist's bossing the patient around. The key portrayal images are, then, the therapist's insistence on showing the patient how to do something and her need to direct the patient. It can be seen, too, that each of these portrayed images contains an implication of the therapist's intervention—that the therapist was unnecessarily pressuring the patient and bossing her around, just as the patient's mother had done in her childhood. (This last reference is an indication of the manner in which the therapist was behaving now in the psychotherapy, that is, in a fashion comparable to the patient's mother in childhood.)

2. We have already identified several of the implications of the therapist's intervention that are encoded in the patient's first dream report. In the second dream narrative, through the use of both displacement and symbolization, the patient encodes the sense of pursuit and attack involved in the therapist's intervention. On a more speculative level, the woman on the horse, as an encoded representation of the therapist, may embody the unconsciously perceived phallic-intrusive quality of the therapist's advice. Further associations from the patient would be needed to validate this speculation.

In the final dream narrative, the patient seems to be representing latent homosexual and seductive aspects of the therapist's noninterpretive intervention. The dream represents the intrusiveness not only as an invasion of the patient's private space, but also as having an incestuous quality. This last dream portrays through condensation additional encoded responses to and representations of the patient's having inadvertently met the therapist's husband.

CLOSE AND DISTANT DERIVATIVES

As we have seen, some encoded representations are easy to decode, and their latent meanings are readily deciphered. Other derivatives are highly disguised and require clever translations and some measure of forced thinking in order to detect their latent meanings. Those derivatives that have been subject to a minimal measure of symbolization or disguise are termed *close derivatives;* those that are heavily encoded are termed *distant derivatives.* In the presence of simple displacement, when the manifest image corresponds to the latent raw image, we have an extreme version of a close derivative—for example, the patient's allusion to a gift he had given his son representing the raw image of his gift to the therapist. Another close derivative, one that contains some measure of disguise, is the woman patient's representation of the therapist's insistent directive (to take her child to the proper physician) by another insistent directive (to pack her van properly). The common theme renders the image readily decipherable. Still greater disguise, though nonetheless producing a close derivative, was in operation when the patient who gave the therapist a gift reported a dream of a woman who wished to hold onto him sexually. Here, a relatively evident implication of the raw image and stimulus is encoded in readily decipherable form; the image of being touched corresponds to that aspect of the gift in which something touched by the patient is then touched by the therapist (in addition, the exchange of the gift itself is a form of touching).

An example of a remote derivative would be this same patient's representation of the therapist's acceptance of his gift by way of a manifest allusion to his boss having to swallow everything that the president of the corporation dishes out. The measure of disguise can be gauged in terms of the degree of evident similarity between the manifest and latent image or theme. Here, the connection is quite remote, in that a surface image of having to take (so to speak) criticism is used to encode the acceptance of a gift. Similarly, if the woman patient whose therapist had directed her to the proper physician had mentioned subsequently that she has a friend who is an advisor at the United Nations, we would have a remote derivative portrayal of the intervention. Here, the shared theme would be advice, an image that deprives the actual raw image of its many threatening qualities.

As one would expect, close derivatives speak for a minimal degree of communicative resistances, whereas distant derivatives or the absence of representation indicate more intense communicative defenses. By and large, communicative resistances are both intrapsychic and interactional products; the therapist's contributions are often significant. Because of this, the rectification of the therapist's contribution to a communicative resistance is a first-order therapeutic task. Beyond that measure, one is advised to give a patient time. Patients in general tend to modify their own communicative resistances as the balance shifts between their need for expression and their need for defense—to the point where they begin to generate naturally material with the potential for decoding and interpretation.

CONCLUDING COMMENTS

To focus for the moment on patients in psychotherapy, it is well to remember that the encoding process is mobilized by dangerous raw images that generate anxiety and reflects a need for both expression and defense. Thus, automatic and unconscious efforts at disguise are mobilized by the very images that stimulate and evoke psychopathology and madness. It is for this reason that encoded derivatives are so intimately connected with the nature and meanings of symptoms and other forms of psychopathology. This understanding also helps to account for the communicative finding that the major factor in the unconscious selection of a representational symbol (i.e., of the manifest derivative that will express an underlying meaning) is the patient's madness itself. Thus, raw unconscious perceptions are selectively understood and portrayed in terms of patient-madness, just as raw unconscious fantasies largely reflect the inner emotional dysfunction of the individual. In essence, then, symbols are chosen because they have relevance to the nature of both the dangerous stimulus and the patient's inner madness.

In conclusion, it may be stated again that the unconscious factors in madness are always communicated in encoded form. Their detection and comprehension must be based therefore on a decoding process that undoes the unique and highly distinctive encoding capabilities of the human mind—in essence, the capacity for displacement and symbolization.

Notes

3 Decoding Disguised Messages

METHODS OF DECODING

Therapists have been involved in a variety of self-deceptions about the extent to which they gain access to and interpret the unconscious implications of material from their patients. The most common types of inteventions decode manifest images as though their latent content existed in isolation from the ongoing therapeutic relationship, and as though it were enough for a therapist to understand universal symbolism, psychoanalytic theory, and aspects of the patient's inner mental world and intrapsychic conflicts.

Messages, however, are not created nor do they exist in isolation. The communicative approach holds that they function as communicative-adaptive responses to traumatic and nontraumatic stimuli. Full and true comprehension of these messages cannot be achieved without an understanding of their precipitants. As an encoded response to a particular stimulus (and by way of condensation, particular stimuli), each manifest derivative is inextricably interwoven with the nature of the trigger or context that has evoked the response.

In contrast to what may be termed *isolated decoding*, the approach to disguised messages based on adaptive and interactional considerations may be termed *trigger decoding*. Synonyms for the latter approach include adaptive-context decoding, adaptation-evoking context decoding, and intervention-context decoding. All these terms imply that the effort at deciphering the disguised message involves a full consideration of the raw stimulus for the encoded message—the trigger that has shaped its form and meaning. It is this form of decoding alone that reveals the most cogent and activated derivative meanings contained in a patient's material.

Isolated Decoding

Interventions that fall under the rubric of isolated decoding are commonly believed to imply a therapist's understanding of a patient's unconscious messages, but they fail to achieve that goal. They may be identified, with some overlap, as follows:

Playing Back Manifest Content. Here, the therapist simply repeats the patient's manifest associations, sometimes with a particular emphasis, as though such an intervention implied insight into unconscious factors. By definition, this cannot be the case. For example, a woman patient will report a dream about a vampire and then recall how her mother would invade her bedroom, question her intensely as if to suck her dry, and then abandon her. The patient concludes that her mother was something of a vampire. At this point, the therapist intervenes, stating forcefully to the patient that she does indeed see her mother as a vampire who wants to suck her dry.

In this instance, partly because of the primitive nature of the image and partly because the image appeared in a dream, the therapist assumes that he has identified an unconscious image. Many writers consider dreams to be either the language of "the unconscious" or direct expressions of unconscious images. They fail to recognize that the reported, thus manifest, dream is a conscious expression and, as such, no matter how primitive, the images being described are a form of manifest content materials. The playback described here involves a sequence of conscious thoughts and images and in no way touches upon unconscious material. No matter how primitive the conscious imagery, and regardless of the form it takes—dream, conscious fantasy, or whatever—the repetition of the patient's manifest association does not involve a decoding process, nor does it entail access to the unconscious factors in the patient's madness.

Inference Making. In this type of effort, a therapist draws analogies on the basis of the patient's manifest associations, thus attempting to identify implications inherent in that material. In general, there is no undoing of displacement or symbolization, and such efforts typically are highly intellectualized.

For example, a therapist might suggest to the woman who dreamed about the vampire that the image suggests a hostile and frightening image of her mother. The mother's intrusion into the patient's bedroom might be held to signify an invasion of the patient's private space, and the fear that her mother would suck her dry, understood to imply both an image of the mother as devouring and the patient's fear of annihilation. Were the patient to add that, at times, she was ready to kill her mother, the therapist might conclude that the patient feels quite hostile toward her mother and has murderous impulses as well.

At times, inference making overlaps the isolated decoding of symbols via psychoanalytic theory. A therapist might conclude, for example, that the vampire represents a dangerous, paranoid, preoedipal image of an orally attacking, phallically intrusive, blood-sucking, and incorporative mother either by inferring meaning from the vampire image as an isolated symbol according to psychoanalytic premises, or by drawing conclusions from the patient's manifest associations to the vampire image.

Inference making is sometimes guided by an attempt to infer connections between one set of associations and a contiguous cluster of further associations. The principle applied here is that there is some underlying (unconscious) link between associations that follow one another. This type of formulating is represented in the decoding effort of the patient herself, who connected the vampire image to her mother, thereby implying a view of the maternal figure in vampire terms. Although this type of inference making often entails a repetition of implications that are evident to the patient, the typical formulation tends to be based mainly on a therapist's supposed intuition and knowledge and, as such, is merely an arbitrary reading out of meanings that seem evident to him or her. The irony is that patients are often as adept as their therapists in using these decoding methods—both in reading off manifest meanings and in generating inferences from surface material. In fact, as Gedo (1979) so sadly notes, patients are often far more skillful than their therapists in carrying out such efforts. This is even true of *isolated symbol decoding* (see following).

Isolated Symbol Decoding. Here, the therapist tends to make use of an understanding of symbolism and psychoanalytic theory, proposing a latent meaning to the surface symbol or other manifest content. In other words, messages are deciphered without taking into consideration the stimulus for the message or its implications in light of an ongoing relationship and interaction. At times, this approach may incorporate the undoing of displacement, but this type of latent-content formulation can be accomplished without it and often proceeds on the basis of inference derivatives.

Isolated symbol decoding is inherently attractive to psychotherapists. The formulations generated in this fashion assume that the patient represents a closed, intrapsychic system; decoding of the manifest content is therefore restricted to purported intrapsychic conflicts within the patient, connections between the patient's present experiences and his or her early life history (genetic reductionism), internal issues, such as narcissism, within the patient, and similar lines of thought that involve only the inner world and external life of the patient. The therapist's part in generating the stimuli to which the patient's messages are an adaptive response is not considered. Indeed, there is an inherent measure of defense afforded the psychotherapist in developing isolated formulations, in that the therapist can consistently avoid his or her own contributions to the patient's material. Avoided in particular are valid perceptions of the therapist that may be contained in the patient's associations—especially the failings and problems of the therapist as they have been reflected unconsciously in his or her interventions. In addition, this type of decoding fails to take into account the patient's individual reasons for selecting one manifest image over another.

It appears to be this inherent measure of protection that makes isolated decoding attractive and fascinating to psychotherapists, obscuring not only its limitations, but also its inherent flaws. The difficulty is compounded by the fact that this type of decoding is fashionablc. It proposes to arrive at formulations related to unconscious contents and factors in madness, and it gives the therapist a sense that he or she is indeed working with unconscious communication. In particular, this type of effort is difficult to modify because there is some measure of truth in its premise (after all, a tree may well be a phallic symbol, and a boat may symbolize the mother). The problem is that in isolated decoding such truths are utilized dynamically in the course of a therapeutic interaction as barriers to deeper and far more chaotic underlying truths—a point to which I made reference in Chapter 2, adumbrated by Bion (1977) some years ago. Bion stated, in fact, that such formulations are actually statements known to be false despite their evident truthfulness. This suggests that otherwise truthful statements may operate as lie, or lie-barrier, formulations, functionally serving in a therapeutic interaction as defenses against or distractions from the most pertinent and activated truths of the moment.

To illustrate this point in a simple way, one might consider the following exchange:

"Do you love me?"

"You're so insecure!"

The answer may contain a measure of truth; it may represent a valid insight; but the emphasis on the first speaker's insecurity is in this context operating as a lie. It is designed as a distraction from a far more disturbing and avoided truth that involves the ongoing relationship between the speakers. In similar fashion, all forms of isolated decoding and inference making serve as a means of generating statements that sound insightful, but are functionally false in light of an ongoing therapeutic interaction. Thus, the belief that a particular effort at decoding has credence, logic, or general support does not imply that the decoding effort involves the most cogent meanings of the patient's material at any given time. Communicative studies have shown that in actuality, such formulations do indeed serve as distractions from the ongoing therapeutic interaction and, in particular, as a means of avoiding highly disturbing but valid encoded perceptions of problems in the psychotherapist.

By way of isolated decoding, a vampire could be seen as the phallic-biting mother or an oral, phallic-biting father, and even as a dangerous sibling figure. A dream image or association that involves overindulgence, servants, and running someone's life could be translated into the dreamer's wishes for merger; as would a patient's statement that, at times, he or she would like to be very close to someone, almost inside of them. A patient who said that at times he does not know who he is might be held to be implying identity confusion. A patient's description of a situation in which he insisted that a friend carry out a specific series of tasks exactly as directed would represent for some therapists the narcissistic patient's misuse of the friend as a selfobject. A dream or associations to the Mafia could be said to imply a variety of meanings, such as dishonesty, illicit power, internecine murder, corruption and the like.

Admittedly, careful attention to the patient's additional associations will minimize the arbitrary nature of isolated decoding. But I am not arguing here that isolated decoding is merely arbitrary and without truth. I am arguing that it is an intellectual exercise whose results are functionally meaningless. The greatest flaw in this type of decoding effort is that it purports to decipher messages from within the patient without a full consideration of the stimuli for these messages, and especially those stimuli or triggers that exist within the ongoing therapeutic interaction. Thus, the open interactional system that actually exists between patient and therapist (the adaptive nature of human communication) is overlooked or denied through an erroneous belief in a closed, intrapsychic system contained within the patient.

The Communicative Approach to Decoding

Trigger Decoding. In trigger, or adaptive context decoding, the effort to deciper a manifest message is based on an understanding that such messages are communicative-adaptive responses to stimuli that have, themselves, communicative and other valences. The communicative approach has shown that the most critical stimuli for the encoded messages from patients are the interventions of therapists. When I say "intervention," I mean anything done by a therapist that can constitute a stimulus to which the patient will respond—whether silence or active comment, securing the ground rules or deviating, the attributes of the setting, and so forth. These interventions account for virtually all encoded expressions witnessed in psychotherapy (the exceptions are quite rare), and, in principle, it is the nature and the implications of the therapist's interventions that shape a patient's encoded material in each therapy hour. Thus, a patient's unconscious selection of a displaced figure or event, and of a particular symbol, will depend on two ever-present vectors: (1) the nature of the therapist's intervention in light of the ongoing therapeutic interaction, and (2) the patient's own inner propensities—in particular, the nature of his or her madness.

Adaptive-context decoding has shown that patients first disguise threatening perceptions of their therapists and only secondarily respond with encoded fantasies. Of concern here, however, is the broader principle that truly meaningful decoding—efforts that capture the major truths contained in derivative form in the patient's material (the basic level of unconscious communication)—can be effected and carried out only by taking into account the immediate stimulus for a message, the determinants within the patient, the present therapeutic interaction, and the patient's past history.

Trigger decoding, then, captures the actual intended unconscious meanings contained in derivative form in the patient's manifest associations. It does so because such messages are adaptive responses to stimuli, and the main stimuli entail the interventions of the therapist. It is to be stressed that not all stimuli lead to encoded messages from patients. Traumas that take place outside of treatment tend to lead to relatively manifest responses with little derivative valence. In addition, this statement implies that when it comes to the nature and meanings of a patient's madness, it is the stimuli contained in the therapist's interventions that mobilize the patient's madness-related responses and therefore lead to reactions fraught with derivative or multiple-meaning messages. It follows, then, that the best technique for decoding disguised messages from patients is adaptive context or trigger decoding. All other efforts at deciphering are functionally false and misleading. Only the proper use of trigger decoding will lead to sound understanding of the patient's material and to interventions that will be validated in the true psychoanalytic sense—indirectly, with fresh, new, unique *encoded* material, and leading to an additional surface working through.

Having been introduced to these four methods of decoding material from patients, one can now examine the way in which each method functions when applied to actual clinical material. Through the following exercises, the reader may get a feel for the different ways in which therapists attempt to respond to material from patients, the extent to which each method produces satisfying formulations, and the degree to which each leads to a sense of closure. No effort will be made here to demonstrate in detailed fashion the failings of inference making and isolated decoding, and the validity of trigger decoding (for such data, see Langs 1978, 1982, 1983). Here the goal is to give the reader a sense of how efforts at deciphering manifest material work in practice and to present some broad evidence for the greater validity and utility of adaptive context decoding. The overall purpose is to facilitate the clinical utilization of adaptive context decoding, because it is at the heart of valid listening in psychotherapy.

DECODING: EXERCISE 3.1

This material is excerpted from the psychotherapy of a young woman suffering from a severe depressive disorder. The patient was being seen by a psychologist (female) for once-weekly psychotherapy, and by a psychiatrist (male) twice a month in connection with antidepressant medication. When the patient had the session from which this excerpt is taken, she had recently seen the psychiatrist. She began her session with the psychologist as follows:

> *Patient*: I saw my cousin this weekend. She has a serious drinking problem. She's gone through a lot of money on

> drugs and liquor because her parents have overindulged her. My cousin has been drinking a lot. It must be destroying her insides. She's gone through a lot of money for drugs and alcohol, mainly because her parents have overindulged her—what one doesn't give her, the other does. She wants to come and live with me for awhile. I refuse to take care of her, let her husband do it. She's like a little bird who wants two mothers; one should be enough. And for that matter, at her age, she shouldn't need a mother at all.
>
> My boyfriend just popped into my head. I keep thinking about his being married. He doesn't know where he should settle in, with his wife or me. Somehow I think the whole situation isn't right. He should chose one of us and let go of the other one. Maybe he wants to have two mothers also.

We will approach this material in the four ways of listening and formulating described earlier.

1. Playing back the manifest content: What meanings can be detected on the surface of this material, simply within its manifest contents? Draw conclusions based on the sequence of the associations.

2. Inference making: What meanings can be proposed by extracting inferences from these manifest associations? For example, what implications are inherently contained in references to drugs and alcohol (oral greed, etc.)?

3. What meanings can be derived from isolated symbol decoding of the patient's images? That is, treat the patient's statements as symbols related to the patient's intrapsychic contents and unconscious memories and fantasies. Use the inferences made in answer to question 2. For example, the patient's references to drugs and alcohol might suggest an unconscious fantasy of doing something destructive to her insides, perhaps derived from her experience of an overindulgent mother. (Be certain to undo a measure of displacement and representation.)

4. What meanings can be derived through trigger or adaptive context decoding? (In this effort begin by identifying the main stimulus for the material. Next, undo the use of displacement and representation, and derive meanings in light of the implications of the stimulus. If this proves difficult, answer the first three questions and then read the answers below, which will include, under question 4, an identification of the adaptive context. Once this has been recognized, return to the exercise and attempt this type of decoding. Utilize the trigger as a guide to selecting the meanings (themes) shared by the manifest and latent images. Identify each latent raw image that can be decoded from this material. In carrying out this portion of the exercise, be sure to identify the manifest theme, the meaning that you have extracted from the surface that is connected to the latent level, and the nature of the raw, repressed perception.

5. State the evident differences in the understanding derived from each of these searches for meaning. What flaws can be detected—if any—in each approach?

Answers:

The following appear to be the best answers to the foregoing questions. In all likelihood, the reader will have similar impressions. If differences emerge between the reader's response and the answers provided here, they may be especially noticeable with respect to questions 1 through 3. In part, the basis for these discrepancies is the fact that all forms of isolated decoding depend in significant measure on the knowledge and personal sensitivities of the decoder. In principle, there should be fewer differences among answers derived from the use of trigger decoding.

1. In regard to reading off the manifest content of this material, the following seems pertinent:

a. The material begins with a reference to a drinking problem. The difficulty is linked to internal destruction. There follows a theme of excessive spending and parental overindulgence.

Using the principle that surface associations must be connected in some underlying fashion (a minimal level of inference making), it might be proposed that the images relate to a destructive form of alcoholic intake which stems in part from overindulgent parents. A therapist might point out this sequence to the patient, believing that this special emphasis will give fresh meaning to the material. Note, however, that without developing an inference (for example, that the cousin may be a substitute for the patient—a form of inference making that also involves a measure of isolated decoding), little more meaning can be attributed to these initial associations. What we have here is simply a sequence of manifest themes and images, admittedly rich in content, that have been translated into selected direct statements.

At times, therapists have deceived themselves into believing that the surface richness of the material implies unconscious meaning. Clearly, this cannot be the case. The patient in this excerpt has stated all of the themes and images at issue quite directly and knowingly. Even the connections between her associations are likely to be directly understood by the patient. In principle, then, the playback of manifest content material, however rich in imagery and surface meaning, does not identify unconscious and encoded contents, meanings, or implications.

b. The next segment begins with the patient's reference to her cousin's wish to live with her. The patient refuses to take care of the cousin and suggests that the cousin's husband do so. Next, the patient speculates that the cousin is like a bird that wants two mothers where one should be enough—though at the cousin's age, she adds, she shouldn't need any mother at all.

In this sequence, there is a wish by someone to live with the patient, the patient's refusal, and her relegation of the caretaking functions requested of her to the cousin's husband. There is an analogy to a bird wanting two mothers and a proposal—a corrective—that one should be enough, or better still, none at all.

Here, the surface issues are: wanting to be cared for, a refusal to give such care, wanting two mothers, and a view of such wishes as inappropriate. Here, too, a therapist might play back these themes for the patient and feel that because of the richness of the imagery, some type of hidden or unconscious meaning has been identified. Of course, this is not the case at all. Similarly, although there is doubtless some connection between the cousin's excessive drinking, waste of money, and overindulgence by her parents and the themes that have been identified in this second segment of associations, a suggestion to that effect represents no significant realization of unconscious material. The observation may be accurate, but it is shallow, isolated, and does little to help the therapist (and patient) to recognize the actual, dynamic unconscious implications of this material.

c. Finally, the patient alludes to a married boyfriend, his uncertainty as whether he should live with the patient or with his wife, and the patient's feeling that there is something wrong with the entire situation. There follows another corrective: the boyfriend should choose one woman and let go of the other. Finally, there is a speculation that the boyfriend also wants to have two mothers.

Thus, in her final segment, there is an allusion to an extramarital affair, the man's uncertainty as to whether he should choose his wife or his mistress (the patient), and the patient's feeling that there is something wrong with this situation. There is a reference to the boyfriend's need to choose one woman and to let the other go. There is also a suggestion that the boyfriend, like the cousin, wishes to have two mothers.

Based on this relatively rich imagery, a therapist might play back this manifest material, proposing to the patient that she is talking about an affair, about choosing one of the two women involved, about something being wrong with the situation, and about the boyfriend's wish for two mothers. The therapist might further connect the manifest themes shared by the material related to the boyfriend and the material pertaining to the cousin: Both, according to the patient, wish to be cared for by two mothering figures. This theme could then be connected to the overindulgence of the patient's parents. Although this would already enter the realm of inference making, the therapist might ultimately comment to the patient that the overindulgence of her cousin's parents seems to have something to do with the cousin's wish for two mothers, and further, that the wish for two mothers is also expressed in her thoughts about her boyfriend. Many therapists, in fact, would view this comment as a "decoded" interpretation of an important unconscious meaning inherent in this material. Indeed, it is possible to identify in this way a connection that may not have been recognized by the patient. It is well to recognize, however, that this represents an extremely simplistic reading out of evident ties among the elements of the patient's productions. This reading in no way involves a decoding process and, thus, cannot state a significant unconscious meaning. It can only serve as an intellectualized speculation.

Because this type of direct reading out is relatively easy to accomplish and has been shown to serve important defensive functions for the therapist, the approach is attractive. It also lends itself to the self-deceptive idea that one is working by such formulations with unconscious processes and contents. It is therefore important to recognize the extreme limitations of this approach and the manner in which it remains fettered to manifest contents, entirely devoid of true decoded implications and even of substantial inferences. Once one realizes that this material alludes to complex intrapsychic and interpersonal issues unconscious to the patient, and especially to valid and accurate encoded perceptions of the therapist, one can see that this type of surface reading is highly defensive. It proposes to reveal the truth while functioning as a barrier to the truth (i.e., as a lie-barrier formation). I take up a more extended examination of this issue in the following chapter.

2. With respect to the inferences that one could make from this sequence of association, the following appear to be the most cogent. (As noted, however, the reader may have somewhat different, even richer, impressions):

a. The allusion to the cousin's excessive drinking suggests oral greed, masochistic needs, a loss of control, and more broadly, self-punitive oral needs and conflicts. This image may well represent the patient's projection of her own impulses and fantasies onto her cousin. (This type of displacement may be postulated for all of the allusions to other figures in this material, although this particular point will not be reiterated as we proceed.) In substance, this formulation implies that these pathological needs and conflicts belong to the patient, although they have been attributed to (displaced onto and projected into) the cousin.

b. The image of the alcohol destroying her insides lends further support to the indications of masochistic needs, though the stress now is on bodily anxieties. In more speculative fashion, the image could imply a destructive introject of some kind.

Note that inference making does not involve the undoing of displacement and tends to rely on *evident indirect* meanings. These impressions are expanded by way of metapsychological premises and applied to the patient by invoking the principles of displacement and projection, as though those processes took place straightforwardly. As noted earlier, displacement means the portrayal of one image by another: The patient is talking consciously about situation A, but talking unconsciously about situation B. Inference making does not attempt to locate situation B. It regards the patient almost as an exponent of standard universal conflicts. The patient's mind becomes a kind of changing-house, whereby oral need, for example, becomes translated into manifest references to orally-incorporated substances.

Psychotherapists have experienced considerable difficulty in distinguishing between inference making and true decoding, so it is important to establish a sense of the basic qualities of each process. In general, the former effort tends to generate cliches, intellectualizations, theoretical postulates, implied trends, patterns, and the like. Moreover, such inferences always involve the patient alone (or sometimes direct postulates regarding other individuals in the patient's life) and propositions related to intrapsychic conflict without basic interactional components. True decoding *begins* from these basic intractional components, whose implications will almost invariably constitute another context—what I've been calling situation B. The decoding effort is concerned with the manner in which these implications are expressed or not expressed as encoded elements in the patient's manifest material.

c. The allusion to the cousin's having spent a lot of money on drugs and liquor because of her parents' overindulgence suggests loss of control, a possible quality of grandiosity, a genetic root for these problems, an absence of proper boundaries and limits, and the presence of competition between the parents as to who will overgratify the cousin—what one doesn't give her, the other does. Spending money may be held to have anal implications and even allude to a sense of power. There is also an implication of an identification between the cousin and her parents, and this may, as noted previously, be postulated to embody a statement that may be true for the patient as well.

d. Next, the patient states that the cousin wishes to live with her, that she refuses to take care of this cousin, and proposes, rather, that the cousin's husband do so. Here, there are the themes of dependency, refusal to merge and issues of responsibility for care—let the husband do it. The wish of the cousin to live with the patient may hint at latent homosexual wishes, and the patient's refusal may involve a defense against such homosexuality—a formulation supported by the image of referring the cousin back to her husband.

Those formulations have a familiar quality and seem meaningful and cogent. At times, they seem to touch on unconscious dynamics and genetics, and even to have validating elements. Communicative studies have consistently shown, however, that such statements only involve *evident* truths which function in the therapeutic interaction as untruths—as lie-barrier systems designed to avoid more pertinent, interactional truths of a highly chaotic nature, including encoded perceptions of therapist-madness and counter-transference. The potential of this approach for defensive utilization and the theoretical plausibility of formulations generated in this manner make inference decoding especially attractive to the unwary psychotherapist. The demonstration of these defensive functions must await our application of adaptive context decoding.

e. The allusion to the cousin being like a bird wanting two mothers, and the recommendation of either one or none, may be seen to reflect an excessive maternal need, and recommendations for renunciation and limit-setting. The bird may be viewed as a symbol of a baby, perhaps even of the male or female genitals; it also hints at smallness, helplessness, and yet the omnipotent ability to soar and fly.

f. Finally, there is the allusion to the patient's lover, his need to choose either his wife or the patient, the sense that there is something wrong about the entire situation, and his wish for two mothers as well. Here, we may propose an oedipal triangle, with rivalry between the patient and her lover's wife, although the latter may be viewed as a form of latent sibling rivalry as well. There is a conscious or superego quality to the patient's sense that the situation isn't right, and issues of triumph and favoritism in the notion that the boyfriend should choose one of the two women with whom he is involved. It may be posited that the wish for two mothers has similar implications to those previously noted for the patient's cousin's comparable needs.

In summary, inference-making involves translations, generalizations, and, as a rule, intellectualization. The resultant formulations often have an impersonal quality, although they can be linked to the personal history of the patient when this is known. Many therapists find it difficult to appreciate that such translations do not involve a decoding process, but merely substitute one set of notions, ideas, or images, for another set of notions, ideas, or images. Because these substitute formations usually involve statements derived from psychoanalytic theory, an unconscious meaning or function is believed to have been uncovered. This proposal is not supported, however, by validation in the way of insight or fresh encoded material when interventions based on such derivations are offerred to patients. In fact, the typical response involves inference making and intellectualization by the patient, with little in the way of unique imagery, surprising derivative expression, or conscious insight.

3. Isolated decoding overlaps considerably with inference making. Many of the answers proposed by the reader for this type of effort may have appeared in the foregoing discussion. In general, isolated decoding involves an attempt to unravel symbols and statements related to a patient's intrapsychic conflicts and unconscious fantasies and memories. The therapist indulges in considerable speculation as to the fantasied and genetic aspects of the patient's material, and these are consistently viewed as part of a closed system within the patient (sometimes in interaction with outside figures). No consideration of the open and ongoing interaction with the therapist is attempted.

The following illustrates efforts at the isolated decoding of the clinical excerpt:

a. The first segment regarding the cousin would most certainly be decoded as a displacement from the patient, that is, as the patient's projection of her own needs, wishes, and conflicts onto the cousin. The patient might be held to suffer from poorly managed oral incorporative needs and fantasies, and to have the unconscious fantasy that she has done something destructive to the inside of her body and perhaps her inner mental world as well. One might also postulate an unconscious fantasy of oral and anal greed based on early maternal overindulgence. One might propose a specific etiology in the patient's experience of inappropriately extended nurturing and likely difficulties on the part of the mother in setting appropriate limits and creating appropriate frustrations for her child—the patient. It may be postulated as well that similar difficulties existed in the patient's father.

b. The reference to the cousin's wish to live with the patient may indicate the patient's own unconscious fantasy-wish for proper maternal care and an identification with a maternal figure who failed to offer the patient such nurturing in the past. It might be said to reflect an unconscious longing for a man—a husband—to provide for such needs.

c. The imagery related to the bird and the two mothers may be a portrayal of the patient's unconscious fantasy of herself as a small child with a diminutive phallus. This imagery may also express an unconscious wish for omnipotence or power (the bird's ability to fly) as well as intensive longings for maternal care, condemned in part by the patient's superego, which proposes a shift toward relative autonomy.

d. The segment regarding the boyfriend might well entail an unconscious fantasy of oedipal triumph over the mother enacted in the relationship with the boyfriend. Here, too, there are signs of superego condemnation as well as intense rivalry and the need for choice. The patient's allusion to the boyfriend's wish for two mothers may reflect the patient's own projected fantasy-wish, indicating that she became involved in the affair because of unconscious longings to possess both her father and her mother, with likely heterosexual and homosexual implications.

As this exercise reveals, isolated decoding alludes primarily to the patient herself, her unconscious fantasies and wishes, postulated genetic connections, and internal conflicts. Because there is no manifest allusion to the therapist in this material, there is no need to formulate the presence of transference or of meaning on any level that pertains to the therapeutic relationship and interaction. On the other hand, if the patient had next associated that she felt jealous of the male patient who preceded her in session with the therapist, one might readily postulate an unconscious fantasy (transference wish) of oedipal need or sibling rivalry and an unconscious wish for exclusive care from the therapist.

In anticipation of adaptive context decoding, it may be stressed again that both inference and isolated decoding fail to consider the stimulus for the patient's material as constituted by the therapist's interventions. As a result, there is virtually no attention paid to unconscious perceptions of the therapist in light of his or her interventions. Furthermore, it is only when the therapist appears in the material manifestly that a formulation is likely to be made regarding the therapeutic relationship. And even then, that relationship is understood only in terms of the *patient's* unconscious wishes, distortions, projections, fantasies, etc.

It is indeed possible to hypothesize a displaced transference wish in this material. Although this would be highly speculative, one could propose through isolated and inference decoding that the patient wishes to devour the therapist or part of the therapist and that she longs to be cared for and overindulged. One might also propose that the patient feels like a small child who is helpless and dependent, and who longs to be cared for by her therapist-mother. One might postulate unconscious fantasies of rivalries with the female therapist's other patients, her husband, or both and longings to be chosen by the therapist above all others.

Notice that the foregoing hypotheses were generated simply by attempting to decode the patient's material in terms of its having been displaced from her relationship with the therapist onto outside figures. Because no attention has been paid to the therapist's interventions, the hypotheses generated in this fashion must postulate longings and wishes on the part of the patient. Distortion may be introduced by postulating that the patient mistakenly believes she has been overindulged by the therapist or, that she has projected a past image of both her mother and father onto the therapist in the present—another transference formulation. In similar fashion one could suggest that the last segment of the material represents a distorted image of the therapist as being unfaithful to the patient, an image based on the patient's own pathological and greedy needs and stemming in part from earlier experiences with her parents. Here, too, the postulate involves pathological projections and displacements from the past onto the therapist. The emphasis is on wish and distortion. There is no consideration of valid perception, and no sense that the therapist may have overindulged the patient, done something incorporatively destructive, created an actual rivalry, and the like.

4. The key adaptive contexts (therapist-interventions) or triggers for this material are: the fact that the therapist had accepted this patient as a referral from a psychiatrist who was providing the patient with medication, and that the therapist was participating in a treatment experience in which the patient had two psychotherapists. These specific interventions by the therapist are fraught with meaning. (Again, therapist-interventions include every aspect of the therapist's efforts—the setting, silences, verbal-affective comments, and all other aspects of the conditions of treatment.)

In preparing to use this broad adaptive context as the decoding key to the patient's associations, we must understand two aspects of the trigger: (1) its actual structure and form, and (2) its dynamic and other meanings and functions. In exploring the patient's associations for encoded communications, one should first seek out and identify portrayals of the structure of the adaptive context. In this instance, the adaptation-evoking context involves treatment by two therapists, therefore by two caring figures, and the creation of a triangulated relationship that includes the patient. The patient has also been receiving medication from one of the therapists in the form of pills, which the patient swallows.

When the patient is meaningfully working over an aspect of the adaptive context, that aspect will be portrayed in clear (close) derivative form. Of course, it is also possible for the patient to allude directly to the adaptive context. The patient in the present excerpt, for example, might have mentioned the other therapist or referred directly to her medication, in which case there would have been a manifest allusion to the trigger. For the moment, because of the nature of the excerpt, we are concentrating upon encoded representations.

It is relatively easy to identify encoded *portrayals* that relate to the structure of an intervention context. It is somewhat more difficult, however, to recognize representations that encode the *implications* of a given intervention, because this requires attempts to formulate the patient's valid unconscious perceptions—that is, the unconscious registration and encoding of perceived or experienced meanings of a therapist's intervention. Communicative studies have shown that this type of unconscious registration, revealed in derivative form in a patient's association, is virtually always the patient's initial response to an intervention from the therapist. It is only after the registration of such perceptions that the patient responds with reactive fantasies, curative or hurtful efforts directed toward the therapist, conscious and unconscious memories, behaviors, symptoms, and the like. Nevertheless, the core adaptive response to a therapist intervention involves unconsciously *selected* perceptions of actual implications of the therapist's efforts—perception before reaction. Finally, the manner in which the patient selects from the myriad of universal and personal meanings that could be accorded to a given intervention is determined mainly by the nature of the patient's most active psychopathology and madness. In essence, then, the patient's organ of perception is his or her madness.

Decoding in terms of an adaptive context takes into account the stimulus for the patient's material and, more specifically, the influence of the therapist and therapeutic interaction on the patient's adaptive and communicative expressions. It therefore becomes crucial for the therapist to be able to evaluate the implications of each intervention made in order to treat them as communicative inputs—expressive stimuli that shape the patient's direct and encoded responses. A therapist will recognize a patient's valid encoded perceptions of the implications of a particular adaptive context only if he or she has consciously identified the most pertinent meanings of the context for the patient.

It is here of course that a significant difference in the role and functions of patient and therapist becomes apparent. The patient's implicit role in the therapeutic process is to communicate in derivative form, quite unconsciously, perceptions of the therapist, which, registered selectively in terms of his or her madness, reveal the unconscious meanings of the patient's psychopathology. The therapist's responsibility is to be aware of this constellation of meanings and functions contained in his or her interventions and in the patient's material so that this information is manifest and available for direct interpretation.

The material in the present volume, in order to concentrate on the basic aspects of the decoding process, is confined to a general reading of the implications of each therapeutic intervention under study. The exercises rely on each therapist's self-awareness and self-knowledge and the broad understanding feasible through a general knowledge of both general psychoanalytic theory and the analytic theory of the therapeutic interaction. In a subsequent work (Langs, in press) a detailed and elaborate schema will be developed by means of which a systematic analysis of therapist-interventions may be undertaken in all-inclusive fashion.

The reader who has not as yet done so is advised to take into account the two aspects of the adaptive contexts relevant to this excerpt—the presence of two therapists, in the treatment situation, and the psychiatrist's use of medication—and attempt (1) to make a general appraisal of the main implications of these intervention contexts, and (2) to decode the patient's material in light of these meanings. Be certain to identify those derivatives that portray the structure of these interventions (their particular forms will inevitably contain some measure of meaning that should also be identified), and those derivatives that primarily touch upon an unconsciously perceived implication of these treatment conditions.

Adaptive context decoding yields the following meanings from the material in the excerpt (again the reader may be sensitive to nuances not considered here, though most of the broad implications of this material will be identified). We will proceed segment by segment, identifying the manifest theme shared with the latent raw image as a basis for the decoding effort. The decoding of symbols involves the identification of a manifest level of meaning, evident within the framework of the surface context, that transposes meaningfully into the latent context (see Chapter 5).

a. First, the patient says that her cousin has been drinking a lot. In light of the adaptive context of the medication, this image can be seen to represent the structure of the intervention: The surface derivative (manifest context) alludes to drinking and to the cousin, while the latent image (transposed context) alludes to medication and the patient. Displacement has occurred from the patient onto the cousin, and from therapy onto the cousin's life circumstances, in order to create the manifest image. We have undone these displacements by proposing that the cousin represents the patient, and the alcohol, the medication. Embedded in the manifest image is the theme of excessive use, suggesting a latent raw image to the effect that there is something excessive about the offer of medication.

In light of the adaptive context of the two therapists, the surface theme of excessive oral intake may touch upon a more general theme of excessive and evidently destructive oral and other nurturing forms of gratification. On that level, this manifest meaning with regard to the cousin's heavy drinking may be tied to a latent raw image pertinent to the existence of the two therapists by way of a decoded *raw message* such as the following: Having two therapists is excessive and creates a situation of undue and destructive oral, nurturing gratification. This raw image touches on a valid unconscious perception of the presence of two therapists, which is indeed both overgratifying (especially in light of the use of medication) and destructive to the patient and her therapist alike.

To summarize, we have taken the manifest image of the patient's cousin drinking a lot and utilized as our decoding key two adaptive contexts: the use of medication and the presence of two therapists. The surface derivative itself suggested unconscious meanings to each of these contexts, and these unconscious meanings, in turn, were used to decode and undo the disguise used to create the surface image. A shift (a transposition) was made from the surface context to the latent context, using the meanings of each latent adaptive context as our guide.

It was also possible to postulate that through condensation, at least two raw messages are contained latently in this first image, each pertinent to one of the actual adaptive contexts that stimulated this material. The first latent raw message was to the effect that medication is an excessive and destructive method of cure. Because communicating this message directly to the therapist would be dangerous, and because the image itself is a dangerous situation and evocative of anxiety, the patient unconsciously encoded this particular perception into a displaced and symbolized message about her cousin's drinking habits.

Similarly, we were able to detect a latent raw message that also found disguised expression in this first association, one that was organized around the adaptive context of the presence of two therapists: Having two therapists is orally gratifying in a destructive sense. Here, too, faced with a dangerous perception and a dangerous message, and stimulated by some measure of anxiety, the patient resorted to communicative defensiveness through the encoding process. By way of displacement and the manifest use of an allusion to the cousin's drinking problem, the patient was able to sufficiently express this frightening raw perception of her psychotherapist while maintaining a sufficient measure of disguise to satisfy her defensive and protective needs. It is worthy of note that such disguise was also protective of the therapist, who might well have become quite anxious, upset, and defensive had the patient confronted her with the raw messages that we have formulated. In substance, then, the encoding process is unconsciously designed to protect both patient and therapist alike.

(Now that the basic form of the decoding exercise has been established, the reader might wish to carry out this type of decoding for each segment of the excerpt in light of the implications of each of the two adaptive contexts before returning to the answers offered here.)

b. The next image states that the alcohol must be destroying the insides of the patient's cousin. In light of the adaptive context of the medication, this appears to be a straightforward mixture of both perception and fantasy (both truth and distortion). The displacement is from the patient, the psychiatrist, and the medication to the cousin and the consequences of alcohol intake. The raw message says in effect that the medication is internally destructive. If the medication had resulted in side effects, this image would contain an entirely valid perception. In the absence of such effects, the raw message represents both a valid perception (in that the use of medication is internally destructive in a general sense) and a distorted fantasy (there is no physiological reason to believe that tranquilizers usually do internal damage to the body). In the main, the patient seems to be pointing to the destructive influences of the use of medication on herself and on the psychotherapeutic treatment process.

In summary, we have taken a derivative sequence wherein the patient states that excessive drinking must be destroying the insides of her cousin's body, understanding the drinking to represent the medication, and the internal destruction to portray the consequences for the patient's intrapsychic equilibrium and treatment experience. Through transposition of meaning from one context (manifest) to another (latent), we have derived a raw image regarding the destructiveness of the medication to the patient.

In the adaptive context of the presence of two therapists, the manifest derivative image of the destruction to the cousin's insides seems to represent an encoded perception of the way in which the excessive use of two therapists is destructive internally (including mentally) to the patient and to her treatment experience. This understanding relies on recognizing that this type of double-therapist situation is inappropriate and that its inappropriate aspects will be perceived by the patient.

Let us continue in a more concise fashion. The primary goal is to provide the reader with a sense of the type of meanings and understanding that can be arrived at through adaptive context decoding. The specific details of this process, especially the means by which a manifest theme bridges and can be transposed into a latent theme, will be the subject of the following chapter.

c. The next manifest segment, reflecting that the cousin spent a lot of money on drugs and liquor because her parents had overindulged her, and including the comment that what one parent doesn't give, the other does, also lends itself to ready decoding in light of the two intervention contexts at hand. With respect to the medication, the surface themes are waste, an illicit use of street drugs and liquor, and overindulgence. Through transposition, these themes suggest the following decoded raw message: The medication is costly and wasteful, illicit in some sense (patients understand sometimes on a conscious and always on an unconscious level that the ideal psychotherapy is medication-free), and a form of overindulgence. This decoded message has been established by undoing the displacement away from the patient and the psychiatrist onto the cousin and her parents, and by establishing a level of manifest meaning that lends itself to transposition to latent meaning in light of the adaptive context.

As for the two therapists, the manifest derivative themes involve an excessive expenditure of money, the inappropriate intake of drugs, overindulgence, and a specific encoded portrayal of the structure of the adaptive context: The two therapists are represented by the cousin's parents. The decoded raw message could be stated as follows: The presence of two therapists is costly, illicit, destructive with regard to oral incorporation, overindulgent, and a situation in which the pathological gratifications not provided by one therapist tend to be provided by the other.

d. The next segment touches on the cousin's wish to live with the patient, the patient's refusal to take care of her, and the patient's proposal that her cousin's husband do so. In light of the adaptive context of the medication, the key manifest themes appear to be living together, refusing proper care (from the husband), and wishing for someone other than the appropriate person (vehicle) to provide the care. The decoded message in light of the medication context (for which the therapist must assume partial responsibility) is as follows: My being given medication is a means by which the therapist joins me in some type of inappropriate merger (represented by living together). The medication is a refusal to provide proper care and a way of making the drugs the vehicle of therapy rather than using verbal-affective insightful psychotherapy.

In summary, the patient is here touching upon manifest themes of people living together, the refusal to take care of someone and the search for an appropriate caretaking figure. In light of the adaptive context involving the two therapists, these themes can be decoded to obtain the following raw message: Each of my therapists appears to require the other as a supportive or caring figure: Treatment under these conditions is like living together or merging with them.

By engaging a second therapist, each therapist also refuses proper care to the patient and lays off the responsibilities involved onto the other person. Given that the psychotherapist to whom this material was reported was a woman, and the psychiatrist a man, the specific encoded perception appears to be that the present therapist does not wish to take care of the patient and prefers that the psychiatrist do so.

e. The allusion to the bird wanting two mothers can be seen to portray the structure of both intervention contexts: (1) It portrays the medication, by suggesting an attempt to treat the patient with both medication and insight. (2) The two mothers are a thinly disguised representation of the presence of two therapists for this patient's psychotherapy. It may well be in addition that the patient sees each therapist as a helpless child in need of two mothers: the patient herself and the other therapist.

The patient's proposal that one mother should be enough does not decode as a displaced perception because there are indeed two mother-like figures in evidence. Images that do not fit as encoded perceptions are best understood as either fantasy-wishes or corrective models—models of rectification. In this instance, the corrective models seem quite readily decoded: I (the patient) should not be subjected to a psychotherapy with two therapists, but should be treated by one alone. Finally, the patient's allusion to her cousin not needing any mother at all suggests a further thought—that perhaps no treatment whatsoever would be better than treatment by two psychotherapists.

f. The final segment regarding the patient's boyfriend and his need to choose to stay with his mistress or with his wife may be seen as a rather distant derivative of the medication issue. As noted, one implication of the use of medication is that it is experienced by the patient as the basic mode of cure and as an alternative to insight psychotherapy. Patients do *not* unconsciously experience medication as an adjunct to insight treatment, nor as a preliminary tool that will help lead to such therapy. Patients tend to utilize but a single means of adapting to intrapsychic and interpersonal anxieties and conflicts; the offer of medication tends to imply that the drug will be the mode of cure—thereby setting aside the pursuit of insight or restricting it considerably.

In this light, the suggestion that the boyfriend choose between his mistress (the patient) and his wife may be seen as an encoded corrective to the therapist regarding the nature of the patient's treatment modality. We arrive at this formulation by recognizing that medication and the interpretation of free associations are two competing modes of treatment; because the patient and her therapist have not selected one or the other, the image of the boyfriend selecting the patient or his wife cannot be an encoded perception of the actual state of affairs in the treatment situation. In contrast, the patient's comment that the whole situation with the boyfriend isn't right is indeed an encoded, though intellectualized, perception of the disturbance in the treatment situation caused by the use of medication. The boyfriend's wish for two mothers reflects the wish in both of these therapists for two treatment modalities: dual-therapist psychotherapy and the use of medication.

Through condensation, the same segment of material contains a series of encoded perceptions and correctives in regard to the

> patient's treatment by two psychotherapists. Here, the manifest themes are more readily connected to the latent raw message, which may be stated in summary as follows: My two therapists appear to have something like a marital relationship, and they are offering me (the patient) an illicit affair with one or the other therapist. I should be provided with a choice to work with one of the therapists, and drop the other. This is because there is something fundamentally wrong with the situation as it now stands. Presently, I am being provided with two mothers, and this (by implication, based on the earlier allusion to an identical image) is inappropriate—that is, one should be enough.

In general, communicative formulations restrict themselves to the material at hand. If we look at this segment of associations in its entirety, certain other implications can be derived through adaptive context decoding. We may propose, for example, that the two adaptive contexts, the use of the medication and the presence of two therapists, have in some fashion replicated an early traumatic and pathogenic situation between the patient and her parents. This genetic link is suggested in the allusions to the cousin's parents—a displacement which in all likelihood represents the two therapists in the present (the here and now; Gill, 1979, 1982) and the patient's parents in the past. There are suggestions of early overindulgence or possibly an overreaction to early parental deprivation. There is a hint of an intense childhood oedipal rivalry that is being acted out by the patient to this day. Nevertheless, it is critical to recognize that the proper formulation indicates that the therapist, in some fashion, is repeating with the patient aspects of her early interpersonal disturbances (a form of nontransference)—a formulation that can be developed only in light of the therapist's interventions (adaptive contexts). It would therefore be incorrect to state that these representations are primarily fantasied and transference-based projections from the patient based on earlier genetic experiences in the face of a different and distinctive relationship with the psychotherapist. It is this latter type of formulation that is characteristic of inference making and isolated symbol decoding, but it cannot be justified once one has a comprehensive view of the stimulus-response (interactional) aspect of the patient's material.

5. Throughout the presentation of the answers to the basic questions proposed for this listening exercise, comments have been made regarding the yield of meaning, the flaws in the decoding processes, and the extent to which valid formulations are derived from each of the four basic approaches to patient material. To summarize, the manifest-content playback approach produces formulations that are entirely confined to the surface of the patient's associations and are lacking in encoded meanings and functions, that is, true unconscious implications. At best, surface connections between images and ideas can be established, but virtually nothing can be understood in regard to the unconscious basis of the patient's madness.

Inference decoding tends to be a highly intellectualized exercise, involving direct readings of implications of the patient's associations. In general, neither displacement nor symbolization are undone, but instead, a new set of terms is substituted for the manifest terms and images of the patient's associations. The yield is seemingly meaningful, but the surface appearance here is quite deceptive. In general, it has been found clinically that inference decoding, which results in intellectualized meanings as they pertain to some aspects of the patient's inner mental life or past history, serve functionally as a means of avoiding more disturbing and chaotic truths. These stem from the stimuli of the therapist's interventions, evoking intrapsychic and interpersonal responses within the patient.

Isolated decoding does involve efforts to undo displacement and to decipher disguised messages. The yield here involves psychodynamic and genetic considerations, although they are focused entirely on the patient and formulated in terms of fantasies, memories, and transferences (distortions derived from the past). However, the method is devoid of all consideration of the ongoing therapeutic interaction and of the unconscious implications of the therapist's interventions.

The yield of seemingly dynamic and genetic implications renders this type of decoding highly attractive to psychotherapists. Functionally, it has been shown that this type of effort serves mainly as a defense against realizations pertinent to the ongoing communicative interaction and to the patient's unconscious responses to the implications of the therapist's interventions. Clearly, only adaptive context decoding can get at the full meaning of the patient's material in light of the input from the therapist, the nature of the therapeutic interaction and experience, and the intrapsychic and interpersonal factors within the patient.

Of interest here is the finding that inference and isolated decoding both yield formulations that are, up to a point, similar on the surface in content and meaning to adaptive context decoding. In the former type of effort, however, these meanings are treated as isolated intrapsychic fantasies and memories; while in trigger decoding, these meanings are afforded specificity in light of the implications of the adaptation-evoking stimuli for the patient constituted by the therapist's effort. It is important to recognize that this similarity in surface appearance does not imply an important measure of similarity in the yield or interventions drawn from each of these decoding efforts. Inference and isolated decoding tend to produce general images that pertain entirely to the patient, providing a therapist with a ready means of denying his or her own input into the patient's expression; in particular, the extent to which the patient's material contains valid encoded perceptions of the therapist is entirely lost. Adaptive context decoding is the only means through which both encoded perceptions and encoded fantasies-memories can be formulated and validated.

To briefly illustrate these distinctions, consider the patient's allusion to her cousin's wish for two mothers. The theme, as detected by each of these methods of decoding, touches on a wish for excessive maternal care. In inference decoding, we would propose the presence of excessive dependency; in isolated decoding, an unconscious wish for two maternal figures, four breasts, and the like. It is only through adaptive context decoding that the statement would shift significantly, to the effect that, in light of the presence of two psychotherapists for this particular patient, the patient has encoded the raw perception of the over-indulgent qualities of the actual existence of the two treating individuals. This same form of decoding proposes that it is the patient's own overindulgent and overneedy psychopathology that leads her to characterize this particular selected meaning of the presence of two therapists as a wish for two maternal figures. It is only through adaptive context decoding that a comprehensive statement can be made in regard to the implications of the therapist's interventions as they are selectively perceived by the patient in terms of his or her own psychopathology or madness. As a result, it is only adaptive context decoding that can take into account both the therapist and the patient, including therapist-madness and therapist-sanity as well as patient-madness and patient-sanity. Then, too, it is only through adaptive context decoding that specific raw images can be defined with precision, and the full impact of the therapeutic interaction taken into account.

The main goal of this chapter has been a comparison of various modes of listening and decoding. Clearly, the effort has been made to establish the cogency, validity, and nondefensive qualities of a single method of decoding—trigger decoding. It has been proposed that other forms of decoding permit self-deception on the part of the therapist, are primarily defensive, and are fundamentally in error. For this reason, the balance of this volume will concentrate on the details of adaptive context decoding. We will now turn to a more careful examination of the patient's selection of symbols and the means by which they are best deciphered by the therapist.

Notes

4
Analyzing the Therapist's Interventions

In psychotherapy, displacement by the patient consistently involves the shift away from a raw perception of or fantasy about the therapist onto someone else or some other situation. Once this process is understood, the undoing of displacement becomes a simple matter. All that remains in the decoding effort is the undoing of symbolization, the process by which a raw image is subjected to disguise.

In general, when a therapist is presented with a manifest symbol, it is relatively easy to propose a variety of possible latent meanings. Several factors complicate this decoding effort, however. First, a given narrative will usually contain a multiplicity of themes and sometimes will be quite abundant in this respect. Second, one must determine which particular meaning or image contained in the manifest message is pertinent to the latent content. Third, and most important, the manifest disguised symbol has been created in response to a specific stimulus constituted by an intervention of the therapist. It therefore becomes essential to adopt a two-step decoding process in all instances: (1) *deciphering the latent implications of the therapist's intervention itself,* and (2) decoding the material from the patient in light of the conscious and especially unconscious meanings of the adaptive context (intervention) that has served as its stimulus.

In substance, then, a therapist must unravel the implications of his or her own interventions first, in order to have a decoding key for the patient's material. Failing such an effort, the attempt to decipher a particular symbol is arbitrary and open to undue bias and countertransference-based influence. On the other hand, with the understanding of one's own interventions at hand, there is a clear guiding principle to the determination of a latent meaning contained in a manifest element from the patient.

The use of a particular adaptive context as a guide to decoding the patient's manifest communications must be safeguarded against distortion and the influence of the therapist's psychopathology. First, the therapist should recheck each manifest image for other possible meanings beyond those initially formulated. Second, the proposal of a latent raw image for a manifest element should be developed as a *silent and tentative hypothesis* contingent on support from subsequent images from the patient, thereby producing a derivative complex that coalesces in respect to a particular unconscious meaning. Finally, an actual interpretation to the patient based on a silently validated formulation must obtain fresh confirmation through the emergence of *new encoded derivatives* that reveal unique and unexpected meanings for the themes and issues at hand. In essence, then, a therapist must attempt to validate decoding efforts both before and after an intervention, by way of the patient's continuing associations, examining carefully the patient's responses. Because every effort of a therapist is subject to possible countertransference-based effects, repeated use of the validating process proves essential (Langs, 1978, 1982).

All communication is interactional, a spiraling sequence of stimulus and response, each sequence having conscious and unconscious meanings. For this reason, every discrete effort at decoding must involve the initial deciphering of a trigger, that is, a prior stimulus for the message under consideration. This could lead to an interminable regression in which a message from a therapist is analyzed in light of the trigger in a patient's material, which, in turn, is deciphered in light of the therapist's previous intervention, which itself would require decoding in light of prior material, and so forth. As a consequence, it is essential for practical clinical purposes to establish a specific starting point for the decoding process in a given hour. Clinical experience has shown that this is best done through an analysis of the manifest and latent messages contained in the interventions of the therapist, generating a series of insights that can then be used as a basis for decoding the material from the patient.

The deciphering process used in understanding the therapist's interventions is usually different from that applied to the patient's material. It therefore becomes necessary to first develop the distinctive features of efforts to analyze the work of the psychotherapist before we can turn, in Chapter 5, to the details of decoding the patient's associations and behaviors.

ANALYZING ADAPTIVE CONTEXTS (THE WORK OF THE PSYCHOTHERAPIST)

This workbook has thus far concentrated on subjecting the material from patients to true decoding—that is, on the undoing of the effects of displacement and disguise. Contrary to expectations, this type of effort does not apply to the therapist's interventions unless they are quite unusual, personal, and countertransference-based. Instead, most of the therapist's attempts to understand the manifest and latent implications of his or her own interventions relies on inference making, knowledge of psychoanalytic theory—in particular, the dimensions of the therapeutic experience, and—an understanding of the role requirements of the psychotherapist. Only rarely is there reason to use symbolic decoding in analyzing an intervention from a therapist. That method would be used largely to analyze errant therapeutic efforts containing idiosyncratic images and narrative elements not derived from the patient's material, but from aspects of the therapist's own pathological inner state.

The reasons for the basic differences in how we decipher the patient's associations and the therapist's interventions becomes evident when we consider the nature and function of the communications from each participant to treatment. As stated earlier, it is the patient's role to express him or herself, consciously and unconsciously, in a manner that conveys and reveals in disguised form the unconscious basis of his or her madness. The ground rules of psychotherapy and the structure of the treatment relationship are designed to enhance such expressions, that is, to favor derivative patient-communication.

On the other hand, it is the therapist's role and function to intervene—interpretively and in regard to the management of the ground rules—and to do so in rational, single-message, reality-oriented, nonderivative, direct, fashion. Because the therapist's interventions should be designed to create immediate conscious insight and should be essentially devoid of therapist-encoded messages, their unconscious implications, although inevitable, should be minimal and inferential rather than conveyed by way of idiosyncratic disguised images.

In substance, interventions should be shaped almost entirely by the material from the patient. On the whole, the therapist's function should be to synthesize the patient's associations and to indicate causal connections and unconscious meanings revealed in the scattered elements of the patient's expressions—in essence, to identify the existence of encoded raw images. In principle, then, a valid intervention is *not* an encoded message, but instead a secondary-process, single-message communication. It is only when a therapist introduces idiosyncratic imagery and elements or mistakenly shapes and organizes the patient's material in errant fashion, that unconscious expressions and meanings stemming from the therapist become available for self-decoding. Because an erroneous intervention is a response to the adaptive context of the patient's material (and secondarily, to the material from other patients and to factors in the therapist's outside life), this type of decoding of a countertransference-based intervention should be carried out in light of the implications of the known patient-triggers for the therapist's efforts.

To reiterate, the need to apply adaptive context decoding to the therapist's interventions can be recognized by the presence of idiosyncratic communications from the therapist as reflected in ideas and images not available in the patient's material. The main technical rule is that a therapist should intervene in a given hour solely on the basis of material available in that particular session and not allude to associations and behaviors derived from prior hours unless the patient has done so. All such efforts at recall by the therapist tend to be countertransference-based, highly and pathologically selective, and often prove to contain unrecognized and encoded expressions. In addition, the failure of a patient to uniquely validate an intervention from the therapist by producing further encoded or derivative supporting material suggests that the intervention was erroneous and also dictates a search for encoded allusions. Decoding an erroneous intervention is important for the therapist, because it reveals the unconscious nature of his or her countertransferences and also helps the therapist to understand the implications of that intervention—implications to which the patient will respond subsequently in direct and derivative fashion. Overall, then, the therapist's countertransferences tend to be expressed by way of derivative elements in an intervention, whereas sound therapeutic work is essentially nonderivative in form.

The skillful therapist should be able to identify countertransference-based, idiosyncratic elements in an intervention and to subject them to true decoding in light of adaptation-evoking contexts, stimuli from the patient at hand, and stimuli from other patients. In any case, a therapist should be continually evaluating and reevaluating each silent intervention that he or she prepares to offer to a patient, as well as each comment and behavior actually expressed in a particular hour. There must be a search for implications, unconscious qualities, nonverbal messages, subtle nuances, the presence of empathy and intuition or lack thereof, and implied meanings not evident in the manifest effort. The more knowledge a therapist has of him or herself, of the requisites of the therapeutic setting and experience, and of the patient's conscious and especially unconscious therapeutic needs, the more precise this appraisal will be. It is also important to understand the basic properties of interventions in order to know areas of success and failure.

Aids to Understanding the Implications of the Therapist's Interventions

In addition to the direct and conscious insights that a therapist may have into the ramifications of an intervention, there are two vital aids available to this critical self-assessment process: (1) The patient will unconsciously transform the secondary-process single-message aspects of an intervention into encoded messages, and (2) the implications of encoded aspects of an errant therapeutic effort are unconsciously perceived and registered by the therapist, and they tend to reach conscious expression in derivative form.

The Patient's Response to an Intervention. In responding to each intervention, the patient proves capable of vast unconscious perceptiveness and understanding. Although patients do show rare moments of *conscious* perspective into the hidden meanings of an intervention, the realizations that take place outside of awareness are far more extensive and consistently valid. These latter insights tend to be highly reliable and wide-ranging (though nonetheless confined to certain limits). They are one of the most important resources within the therapeutic interaction. By decoding the patient's encoded perceptions of the meanings and implications of the therapist's interventions (their direct and derivative functions), a therapist may gain considerable understanding of the nature of his or her own work.

In actual clinical practice, a great deal of the therapist's time is spent decoding the patient's selected perceptions and insights into the nature of the therapist's communications. In the presence of errant interventions, the patient's encoded expressions are fraught with valid perceptions, selected from the vast array of universal and specific meanings of a particular therapist-intervention—selected mainly in terms of the patient's own psychopathology or madness. As a result, this type of therapeutic work provides considerable self-insight for the psychotherapist, while constituting a means by which the introjective aspects of the patient's madness can be analyzed and insightfully resolved—the latter through the use of both interpretations of the patient's valid encoded perceptions, and efforts by the therapist to rectify his or her errant efforts.

The Therapist's Response to the Intervention. The second means by which a single-message (and/or encoded) intervention is transformed into derivative expression involves the unconscious response of the therapist. While formulating an intervention or after offering it to the patient, a therapist may experience spontaneous or intrusive images or associations that contain encoded perceptions of the implications of that intervention. During the hour, it may be possible for the therapist to engage briefly in a bit of loose free associations to the therapeutic endeavor. Should he or she choose to do so, additional associations may be generated during a quiet moment during the day or before falling asleep at night. The therapist may even have a dream containing images whose latent meanings entail encoded representations of the implications of the therapeutic effort. In all such instances, the therapist should free-associate loosely, allowing unexpected images to emerge, before engaging in self-scrutiny or analytic efforts. Only then should the therapist try to decode this personal material in light of the adaptive context of the patient's associations and behaviors (the triggers for both the therapist's intervention and his or her later associations).

Great care must be taken, because a therapist is far more vulnerable to the influence of distorting psychopathology when attempting to decode his or her own encoded messages than when attempting to decode material from the patient. Finally, it is only nonvalidated interventions and those that appear to be especially disturbing for the particular patient, the therapist, or both, which should be the eventual focus of adaptive context decoding. In contrast, the decoding of the patient's unconscious perceptions and the implications of the therapist's interventions, obtained by way of derivative messages from the patient, is a consistent part of the therapeutic endeavor with the patient in each and every session.

MEANINGS OF INTERVENTIONS: EXERCISE 4.1

Understanding the latent meanings of an intervention ultimately depends on the therapist's self-knowledge and knowledge of psychoanalytic theory, including concepts related to the therapeutic interaction in particular. It is possible to comprehensively examine each intervention made in light of the seven dimensions of the therapeutic interaction (Langs, 1982; see Appendix), but for the purposes of the present exercises, the reader should rely on general clinical impressions. Each intervention presented should be examined as a potential encoded message for elements that contain derivative meaning and can be decoded in light of the stimuli of the patient's material. In addition, the important direct and indirect meanings of the intervention should be identified as critical implications that may engender a patient's unconscious response. This process of identification, as indicated, does not entail a decoding effort.

In the following exercises, identify the most critical encoded messages and implications in each therapist's interventions. The answers provided will focus on those indirect implications and decodable images which appear to be most pertinent. Thus, at times, the reader will no doubt postulate meanings not covered in the text. If the reader is satisfied with the relevance and cogency of his or her formulation, these meanings can be tentatively accepted as valid. Occasionally, additional material from a patient will permit a reader to validate a formulation not included in the answers.

The following material is a condensation of several different therapeutic experiences. In each instance, the material from the patient was similar, but the intervention from the therapist was quite different. Thus, the exercise allows for a contrast of selected styles of intervention.

The patient is a young man who began his session as follows:

> *Patient*: I would like you to change the time of my hour next week, because I have an appointment with my dentist and it conflicts with the time of my session. (Silence.) Somehow, I'm now thinking of how my mother overindulged me when I was a child. She would grant my every request; she seemed fearful of saying no to me even when it was appropriate for her to do so. In some way, this must have contributed to my drinking alcohol so much. She really shouldn't have spoiled me that way.

This is the material to which each of the therapists responded. We will take each intervention and examine it separately, asking the same two questions about each therapist's effort: (1) Does the intervention contain an encoded message? and (2) What are the main implications of the intervention?

Since our focus is on unconscious communication, the first implications to be identified for each intervention should deal with the manner in which the intervention reflects the level and type of listening process adopted by the therapist, and the ways in which the intervention is likely to influence the patient's own communications.

> *Therapist 1*: I understand that you are requesting a change in your hour next week. The reason you offer for making the change makes sense to me, and I will, towards the end of the session, propose a different time for our meeting next week.

In respect to the intervention by this therapist, answer the following questions:

1. Is there an encoded message here? If so, state the likely raw (decoded) latent message and identify the means by which you arrived at the underlying meanings.

2. What are the main *implications* of this intervention?

Answers:

1. This intervention appears to be largely nonderivative in nature, and it contains little encoded meaning. The therapist is

simply stating that he will accede to the patient's proposal and change the time of his session for the following week. The therapist's response is in keeping with the patient's manifest request, an aspect that tends to favor single-meaning content. There is no evidence of displacement or symbolization.

2. The following appear to be the main implications of this intervention:

a. The therapist is not attending to and does not understand the patient's derivative material.

b. This intervention reflects manifest content listening and a failure to consider the patient's derivative material. In this way, the therapist reveals himself to be derivative deaf.

c. Surface-oriented interventions tend to promote single-message expressions from the patient (in principle, manifest-content therapists unconsciously pressure the patient toward nonderivative communication).

d. The ideal ground rule, that a patient should be responsible for all sessions and that the hour should not be changed, is violated by this intervention. All such deviations, imply poor holding and containment of the patient by the therapist; in this particular situation we may assume damage to the interpersonal boundaries between patient and therapist (the therapist is overgratifying the patient) and disturbances in reality testing (the therapist is uncertain as to the exact day and time of the session, a confusion that the patient will also experience, disturbing his own contact with reality). In addition, this particular deviation reflects a poor capacity on the part of the therapist to maintain controls, a meaning that is often reflected by many breaks in the frame.

e. The therapist is overgratifying the patient in a manner similar to that of the patient's mother in childhood, the implication being that the therapist is offering the patient a pathological symbiosis.

f. The therapist is intervening by way of action rather than by analyzing, and he is reinforcing symptom alleviation by way of action-discharge rather than by insight.

g. The therapist is afraid to frustrate the patient, likely anticipating the patient's hostile response to such frustrations.

h. The patient is using the therapist as a narcissistic selfobject for manipulation and omnipotent control.

i. Given that the intervention is essentially unsound and a reflection of countertransference, it is also an act of madness.

In summary, the most powerful implications of this intervention involve the failure to attend to derivative meanings, the violation of a ground rule, the overgratification of a patient, which repeats the pathological interaction that existed between the patient and his mother, and a stress on mad action-discharge. The intervention, while fraught with pathological implications, does not, however, contain an idiosyncratic, encoded communication from the therapist. The unconscious aspects of the intervention involve implications rather than encoded messages. Nevertheless, recognition of the main attributes of the therapist's effort would facilitate the decoding of the subsequent associations from the patient—would, in essence, serve as a key for deciphering the patient's responsive material (much of it in the form of selected, valid, unconscious perceptions of the therapist in light of his interventions).

> *Therapist 2*: You have mentioned your mother's overindulgence and your own excessive intake of alcohol. These images seem to suggest that you have a strong identification with your mother and that you view her as a dangerous, devouring orifice—a mouth or a vagina.

Again, answer the following questions regarding the intervention by this therapist:

1. Is there an encoded message here? If so, state the likely raw latent message and identify the means by which you arrived at the underlying meaning.

2. What are the main implications of this intervention?

Answers:

1. The therapist has introduced manifest images not contained in the patient's material. Because they are idiosyncratic, and because they take the form of narrative or image content, they are likely to contain truly encoded (displaced and symbolized) meaning. The image centers around the view of the mother as a dangerous, devouring orifice—a mouth or vagina. Because we lack the therapist's associations, we can propose only highly speculative latent meanings. These would require confirmation from the therapist's own responsive thoughts and feelings. Nonetheless, in principle, it seems safe to state that the images offered by the therapist have the potential to convey displaced, latent (encoded) contents.

In this respect, it should be noted that even though the patient's associations may justify private speculations of the kind proposed by the therapist, there are no encoded representations in the patient's material of a devouring mouth or vagina. This intervention therefore reflects a *conscious* idea or fantasy on the part of the therapist, with likely latent meanings. It is evident that there must be a measure of displacement here, because the therapist is probably referring to his own mother and a fantasy that he possesses, rather than to the patient's mother and an unconscious fantasy harbored by the patient (even if the patient does harbor an unconscious fantasy of this kind, it is not expressed in this material and is therefore proposed to him prematurely and arbitrarily). The therapist has taken a rather general image of the patient's mother and has seized the opportunity to project into the patient a conscious fantasy on his part regarding his own mother. In substance, the therapist has stated and encoded his own fantasy by attributing it to the patient.

Proposals regarding the raw message contained in the therapist's intervention are more difficult to formulate. The image itself is quite raw, though it must in principle be an encoded version of a still more threatening image. It may well be that this is the therapist's unconscious image of his patient, and that this particular intervention expresses the raw image as follows: I (the therapist) am fearful of you (the patient) as someone who wishes to devour me orally or anally.

Here, a conscious fantasy regarding a woman/mother contains a latent fantasy regarding a man/patient/(latently) father. It is also likely that there is an unconscious sexual component latent in this image, one that could be embodied in the following disguised raw message: I (the therapist) am fearful of sexual congress with women, because I believe that I will be devoured through fellatio or vaginal intercourse.

Another common unconscious fantasy that may well be reflected in this intervention would involve a displacement from the therapist himself onto the patient's mother. Here the raw image (the decoded or unconscious fantasy) would be as follows: I (the therapist) am a devouring orifice (a mouth/vagina) who listens in destructive fashion to you (the patient) and others. I am identified with my own mother in this respect.

Although there are indeed other possible latent meanings encoded in this manifest intervention, the present discussion has been developed mainly to offer a model of decoding that can be applied to such efforts by the therapist. This therapist should have recognized in retrospect that he had introduced an image not contained in the patient's associations. Of course, it would have been better, if the therapist had been aware of his own wish to make an idiosyncratic contribution to the patient's material before verbalizing it in the session; but retrospective awareness can guide the therapist toward self-analysis. On this basis, the nature of the error may be understood, the therapist's unconscious communications identified, and a decoding key developed with which to comprehend the patient's responsive behaviors and associations.

Upon recognizing his or her error, the therapist should seek out the immediate adaptive context (the trigger) for his or her communicated image. By analyzing the implications of the patient's prior material, the therapist would then have a decoding key with which to decipher his or her own encoded communications to the patient. This might well lead to a valid interpretation to the patient based on the latter's selected encoded perceptions of the therapist's effort, so, as noted earlier, it would be well for the therapist to leave to a quiet moment any effort to engage in further associations to this mistake or to carry out a more extensive endeavor at self-analysis. These specific efforts at decoding can be supplemented by recognizing the additional implications inherent in the intervention at hand. In general, it is alterations in the ground rules of psychotherapy and the communication of encoded messages introduced by the therapist that have the greatest impact on the patient. Thus, undertanding the encoded implications of such expressions as well as their general meanings provide an important basis for the understanding of a patient's responsive associations.

2. As for the general implications of this intervention, the following appear to be most pertinent:

a. In regard to listening, there is a failure to offer the intervention in terms of the patient's own material. Both the patient's manifest contents (the request to change the hour) and the evident derivative meanings (the latent contents) are ignored. Instead, the therapist imposes his own imagery on the patient's material, projecting and projectively identifying into the patient his own conscious and unconscious perceptions and fantasies. In substance, the therapist unconsciously behaves here as a *functional patient*, requesting therapeutic help from the *designated patient*, who is asked to adopt the role of *functional therapist*.

b. There is a failure to manage the ground rules of therapy at the behest of the patient's derivative directives. The patient will view this problem as poor holding and containment.

c. In the therapist's failure to understand the patient's material and to respond in terms of the level of expression from the patient, there is an autistic mode of relatedness—in a form of interpersonal withdrawal—on the therapist's part.

d. Though words are in use, the intervention is a form of action-discharge rather than an effort to afford the patient a measure of true insight. The projective identification involves anxieties, fantasies, and perceptions related to the therapist's own inner mental world and conflicts, especially as they pertain to his relationship with, and introjects of, his mother.

e. The therapist introduces his own annihilation and bodily anxieties into the treatment situation.

f. The therapist uses the patient as a selfobject for his own pathological needs.

g. Because of its idiosyncratic and primitive nature, the intervention has a quality of expressed madness.

In the actual clinical situation, a given patient may find it necessary to cope with several interventions dominated by a therapist's countertransferences at one particular juncture. At such moments, the therapist must be capable of selecting the most cogent and deviant of his or her interventions for the patient, and of recognizing the most powerful and pertinent latent meanings contained within these efforts. In this way the best guide for decoding a patient's subsequent associations is created.

> *Therapist 3:* You have asked me to change your hour next week. Notice that you then went on to talk about your mother's overindulgence and how it contributed to your own excessive use of alcohol. In this way, you seemed to be stating indirectly to me that should I comply with your request, I would be viewed by you as overindulging you in a manner comparable to your mother's destructive behavior with you in your childhood. Indirectly, you are trying to tell me that such a response—changing your hour—would support and further contribute to your problems with overuse of alcohol. In addition, if I were to change the time of the session, you would see me as fearful of frustrating you even when it is appropriate that I do so. In fact, you yourself have provided us with the answer to your request through your statement that your mother should not have spoiled you in that way. Clearly, you are suggesting that I should not spoil you by changing your hour, lest I overindulge and spoil you as your mother did in the past and lest I support your excessive use of alcohol in the present.

In considering this intervention, answer the following questions once again:

1. Is there an encoded message here? If so, state the likely raw (decoded) latent message and identify the means by which you arrived at the underlying meaning.

2. What are the main implications of this intervention?

Answers:

1. This therapist has adhered closely to the material from the patient. He has not introduced an image of his own into the patient's associations and has, in essence, attempted to synthesize the patient's associations into an understanding of the unconscious meanings of his request for a changed hour and the consequences should the therapist comply. Thus, this intervention is primarily an effort at decoding rather than the transmission of a fresh, idiosyncratic encoded message from the therapist. It is this type of expression that constitutes a sound interpretation.

2. There are two components to this particular intervention: (1) adhering to a ground rule of psychotherapy which states that the patient is responsible for all sessions and that they should be held at a fixed time, and (2) the offer of interpretive insights as to the unconscious meaning of the request and the consequences of the therapist's compliance. The main implications of this effort are:

a. The therapist has understood and utilized the patient's encoded expressions and therefore reveals a sensitivity to unconscious communication. This implies a capacity to understand the unconscious basis of the patient's madness and to use encoded directives from the patient in managing the ground rules of the psychotherapy. Implicitly, the therapist is also encouraging further multiple-message (derivative) communications from the patient and indicating that he is prepared to deal further with the underlying basis of the patient's psychopathology.

b. At the behest of the patient's derivative directive, the therapist has indicated that he will adhere to the ground rules of psychotherapy—that he will hold the frame. Implicit in such an effort is a basically trustworthy image of the therapist as someone who can be relied on to not overindulge the patient, to maintain proper interpersonal boundaries, to possess sound reality testing, to represent clear ground-rule realities, and to hold and contain the patient in a constructive manner. In addition to this sense of safety, however, the patient will also experience as a consequence of this intervention the confining qualities of the ground rules of treatment; he is therefore likely to feel claustrophobic anxieties as well.

c. This intervention is an offer of a constructive insight, a sound interpretation. As such, it speaks for cure through understanding and holding, rather than through action-discharge. It is an intervention likely to be validated by the patient's subsequent material.

d. Interventions of this type reflect the sanity of the psychotherapist, his ability to metabolize the patient's communicative expressions toward understanding and, thereby, to forego pathological satisfactions, and to function primarily in the service of the patient's therapeutic needs.

An analysis of the decoding process utilized by this therapist will prepare us for the exercises in the following chapter, which concentrates on the deciphering of the patient's symbolic representations. For the moment, we do not know the trigger or stimulus that prompted the patient to request a change in his hour. Such issues usually arise either when the therapist has secured the ground rules of psychotherapy by way of a recent active intervention or when the therapist has acceded to another deviation. Because the trigger was actually somewhat different in each of the cases that I condensed into one patient-excerpt, we will adopt a different decoding effort in order to maintain uniformity. This clinical excerpt touches upon one of those rare situations in which one of the crucial adaptive contexts is an anticipated intervention, namely, the expectation that the therapist will indeed shift the time of the session. We will therefore utilize this potential trigger as the organizer of our decoding effort.

In analyzing the intervention of the first of the three therapists cited, we have already identified the main implications of this intervention context, stressing its pathologically gratifying aspects. We may therefore return to the patient's material in order to treat the segment as a potential derivative message that requires a decoding effort. We may undo displacement by applying the validated concept that all of the images have been displaced from the therapist onto someone else—here, the patient's mother. With the displacement undone, we can adopt a preliminary, general monitoring decoding effort. We simply apply the surface messages and themes (without attempting to undo symbolization for the moment) to the therapist, proposing that their meanings contain valid perceptions of the implications of the therapist's effort before considering possible fantasy formations. Thus, the patient's associations suggest that the therapist has overindulged the patient, unnecessarily granting a prior request for fear of frustrating him even when appropriate. It is this gratification that supports the patient's excessive intake of alcohol.

Next, we take the adaptive context of the anticipated change in hour and apply the sequence to the implications of that particular intervention. We therefore would hypothesize that the patient is stating that a change in session of the kind he is proposing is an overindulgence and will be carried out because of a fear of reasonably refusing the patient. Such behavior lends support to the patient's own need to overindulge himself—his psychopathology.

Next, we may state the dangerous raw-image perception of the therapist contained in disguised form in this material: If you change my hour, it will be an overindulgence carried out because you are afraid to refuse me. I will consider (and introject) your own need to overindulge me as support for my need to overindulge myself through drinking. To this, we may now add the final piece of the sequence—the patient's comment that his mother should not have behaved that way. Thus, the raw message would conclude: I (the patient) am advising you to maintain the schedule as it now stands; you should not overindulge me as I requested and as my mother once did.

In this instance, the patient's images are general and do not involve a specific narrative. As a result, the decoding process is rather limited, and there is little sign of symbolization. However, the patient's allusion to his own excessive alcohol intake must also be taken as a separate encoded message. In light of the anticipated adaptive context, what is its raw meaning?

One of the attributes of a therapist's decision to change the time of a session involves the need to establish a pathological symbiosis with the patient. Among the qualities of such a symbiosis, especially when overgratification is involved, is that it has addictive properties. The patient perceives the therapist to be using him as a selfobject and wishing to entrap or incorporate the patient for his own pathological needs. Thus, the encoded raw message that could be deciphered from the patient's allusions to his own excessive intake of alcohol might be stated as follows: If you (the therapist) change the hour, it is because you have a pathological, addictive, incorporative need for me that is inherently self-destructive.

MEANINGS OF INTERVENTIONS: EXERCISE 4.1a

To complete this illustration, we may consider an additional segment of associations offered by one of these patients. After stating that his mother should not overindulge him as she did, he spoke as follows:

> *Patient:* I remember now when my mother was depressed, she would stuff me with candy and soda. Somehow, this leads me to think of this friend of mine who cut back his psychotherapy from twice to once weekly; it was a disaster.

Using the adaptive context of the anticipated change in the patient's hour, how would you decode these two message segments?

____

____

____

____

____

Answer:

This first segment makes reference to the mother's depression and to her stuffing the patient with candy and soda. We may undo the displacement by stating that the latent images allude to the therapist, implying of course that the patient has used his mother for such a representation. Specifically, the patient indicates that he would perceive the therapist as depressed if he were to change the hour. This perception is justified by the realization that such a move reflects an unconscious need in the therapist to overgratify the patient, one that is likely to be based on a sense of deprivation and depression-related wishes to be overgratified himself. The fear of frustrating the patient and the need to gratify his pathological needs also suggest depressive trends in the therapist, who is unable himself to tolerate the frustration and separateness (loss) involved in adhering to the established ground rule. Thus, this particular encoded message basically utilized displacement with little additional disguise.

This image involving depression touches on a valid, dynamic implication of the therapist's potential intervention. Had the patient stated this reading of the therapist's effort consciously and directly, he would have been seen as a bright and sensitive diagnostician. This is the case because of the relative absence of the use of symbolization. It is impressive to realize the capabilities of the naive human mind when it functions and communicates outside of immediate and direct awareness.

The image of being stuffed with candy and soda does, on the other hand, reflect the use of the symbolization (representation) process. In light of the adaptive context of the potential change in the time of the patient's session, the candy and soda represent inappropriate indulgences, harmful gratifications. That latent allusion is to the overindulgence and harmful qualities of the shift in time. In this instance, a particular attribute of the adaptive context is symbolized in terms of inappropriate oral satisfactions. The particular choice of symbol appears to have been determined in part by the patient's own pathological, oral-greedy needs and his problems with impulse control. In addition, the perception is stimulated by one of the universal meanings of this type of shift in hour—it is indeed an overindulgent, pathological, symbolic oral gratification of the patient. Thus we see once again that a communicated encoded perception from a patient is determined by the nature of both the adaptive context and the patient's madness. These are the determinants of the selection of a specific symbol used by the patient to represent a meaning of an intervention by the therapist.

In all, this particular segment may be decoded into the following dangerous raw image-message: If you change the time of my session, it will reflect your own depressive state. You will be overindulging me and providing me with an inappropriate and frivolous form of inappropriate oral satisfaction.

The second segment makes reference to a friend's decrease in the frequency of psychotherapy sessions. Here, the friend's therapy represents the patient's therapy through displacement. The decrease in the frequency of sessions is the disguised representation of (the symbol for) the change in the hour. The allusion to the disaster is an encoded perception of the consequences of the shift in the time of the session. The underlying raw message is as follows: If you change the time of my session, it will have disastrous consequences.

In this instance, displacement is at work throughout. One element of the patient's message is also symbolized. The change from twice weekly to once weekly deals with the general theme of alterations in the basic ground rules and conditions of treatment. Thus, the ground rule of a set frequency of visits is used here to represent a different ground rule—the one pertaining to the time of the sessions. One manifest tenet is used to encode another. Finally, the reference to disaster is an unencoded implication, a general image of the consequences of all such deviations.

CONCLUDING COMMENTS

The key to understanding the material from patients is self-knowledge and, in particular, the therapist's awareness of the implications of his or her own interventions. To know the patient, the therapist must know him or herself. The material from patients, once viewed as isolated intrapsychic products and expressions of transference and fantasy, must be understood as communicative adaptive responses and as efforts mainly to cope with the therapeutic relationship and interaction (and with outside traumas through the vicissitudes of this relationship). There is no understanding the complexities of a patient's material without a full comprehension of the intricacies of the therapist's interventions.

In principle, the following can serve as a guide to self-understanding and to an analysis of each and every effort by a therapist:

1. In listening to a patient, silently formulate tentative interventions before offering them to the patient. Seek out silent validation for the hypotheses you are developing. Subject the entire proposed effort to derivative validation before offering the intervention to the patient. In particular, attempt to recognize idiosyncratic elements or mistakes in formulations with respect to meaning and function.

2. Once an intervention is offered to the patient, the therapist should reanalyze its content and functions. Here, too, attention should be paid to signs of possible error.

3. If an intervention is not validated by way of derivatives contained in the patient's responsive associations, the therapist should intensify his or her search for deviant aspects of that intervention.

4. The effort should be made to understand the nature and functions of each intervention—its conscious and unconscious implications—in as comprehensive fashion as possible. Toward this end, the seven dimensions of the therapeutic interaction (Appendix) serves as a useful guide.

5. Each intervention should be subjected to immediate self-analysis by means of which the therapist identifies prominent inputs. For those interventions that receive no validation, that contain idiosyncratic elements, and appear to express countertransference-based encoded messages, the therapist should allow time for subsequent free association, the development of encoded unconscious communications pertinent to the meanings of the errant effort, and analysis of these encoded messages. In addition, the patient's associations, because they embody encoded unconscious perceptions of the ramifications of the therapist's efforts, should be used as a major resource for the discovery of initially unrecognized implications to the therapist's work.

6. The therapist should be mindful of those interventions which are likely to have the greatest impact on the patient, because these will be major determinants of the patient's reactions and material. In general, alterations in the ground rules of psychotherapy are the most powerful adaptive contexts for patients, although noninterpretive interventions and therapeutic efforts containing idiosyncratic encoded images are also important.

7. The key to this type of self-analytic work by the therapist is the identification of the adaptation-evoking stimuli in the patient's immediate material, which provided the trigger for the therapist's errant (or valid) response.

Because of the spiraling communicative interaction that occurs between patient and therapist, it is the patient's behaviors and associations that offer the best means to the therapist for the recognition of previously undetected implications of his or her therapeutic work. Thus, a therapist's self-comprehension, which serves as a basis for understanding the patient's material, is actually enhanced by the decoding of those very associations. The patient does much to help the therapist function well in his or her role. In return, the therapist offers a valid interpretation or a framework-management response, synthesizing what the patient can generate in fragmented form on an unconscious level, but is unable to develop in direct fashion. It is the absence of this conscious and directly adaptive resource that leaves room for and defines the work of the effective psychotherapist.

Notes

5
Decoding the Material from Patients

We may reiterate the principles necessary for decoding the material from the patient:

1. Identify a manifest *theme*, extracting it from the manifest content.

2. Identify the *trigger* or adaptive (intervention) context (the latent context) that has evoked the theme.

3. Recognize the main implications of the trigger.

4. Delineate all levels of meaning contained within the manifest theme.

5. Undo the use of displacement by substituting the adaptive context (the latent context) for the manifest context (the surface narrative framework).

6. Use a meaning of the adaptive context to select the particular aspect of the manifest theme that belongs to the latent image or raw message. Be as specific as possible within the limits imposed by the associations at hand from the patient.

7. Transpose the theme and meanings selected from the manifest content to the latent context by using a selected implication of the adaptive context as the guide.

8. Generate a (decoded) statement of the latent raw image and message that had been encoded into the manifest associations.

The first step to decoding, then, lies in the identification of themes inherent in a manifest message. This effort may involve various types of abstractions or may be quite concrete. The manifest theme exists within a particular surface context and has a definitive—usually single—meaning within that framework. Nonetheless, the same theme also belongs to a latent context. Within this second framework, the theme has an implication either similar to or somewhat different but related to its main meaning on the direct level.

Thus, the central issue in decoding involves the ways in which a given surface image contains a variety of meanings. One particular meaning may be critical to the manifest message, while a similar or a different meaning will be critical to the latent (adaptive) context. The surface theme shifts function and is transposed in light of the latent configuration. In psychotherapy, the latent or second context is always an aspect of the therapeutic relationship, situation, and interaction. Decoding therefore involves as its central process the *transposition* of a manifest theme to a latent (therapeutic) context and meaning. Because encoding transposes a latent and unconscious raw image into a manifestly expressed encoded content, the decoding process simply undoes the displacement and symbolization involved, permitting recognition of the originally threatening raw image and message. In human communication, encoding is essentially a matter of the transposition of themes (displacement) and the use of a measure of disguise (symbolization).

We will now turn to a series of exercises designed to familiarize the reader with the decoding process in psychotherapy, rendering such efforts both workable and understandable.

DECODING MATERIAL: EXERCISE 5.1

Consider the following message from a woman patient in psychotherapy:

Patient: I drank a glass of water.

Here is a brief message in isolation. For the present exercise identify as many themes as possible contained in this image. Be sure to include both concrete and abstract or general themes.

Answers:

1. Concretely, drinking may allude to just that: oral incorporation. Thus the first theme is of taking in something orally. The something—again, on a concrete level—is a glass of water. The first theme combines drinking with taking in water.

2. Drinking is a form of oral incorporation and touches thematically on all types of incorporative acts—for example, eating, swallowing, and ingesting other substances. The image of taking in via the mouth may represent (encode) incorporation by way of any of several orifices—nasal, anal, aural, and even visual.

3. Another abstract meaning involves taking something external into one's own body or, more broadly, placing it inside of oneself. Here the something may be an image, an idea, a trait belonging to someone else, or any other type of psychologically incorporative transaction.

4. In addition to its concrete meaning, a glass of water may represent any type of liquid as well as any form of nourishment. A related theme involves relief-giving substances.

5. The glass may concretely represent a specific glass or various classes of glasses. The glass may also convey the theme of containers, whether for water and other forms of nourishment, or for any other substance. As such a container, the glass could also represent inanimate objects that contain, as well as the containing aspects of the total human body or its specific containing organs—for example, the mouth, anus, stomach, and so forth. The glass may also allude to psychological forms of containing and containment.

6. The glass may touch upon the theme of fragility, because glass is breakable and has the potential to shatter.

This exercise demonstrates how a simple message may carry a wide variety of themes, some of them interrelated, extending from the concrete to a variety of abstractions. In this instance, the drinking may symbolize various kinds of incorporative acts; the glass may represent different kinds of containers; and the water may allude to a myriad of substances. The entire message seems to stress a relief-giving incorporative act, although this overall expression need not be the most central implied—latent—meaning intended by the message sender. In psychotherapy, the selection of the most pertinent manifest themes to link up with (bridge and transpose into) the latent context is determined, as noted, by the implications of the activated adaptive context and the nature of the patient's own madness.

To continue this exercise, answer the following questions:

Name at least three interventions to which this message could have been a response. For each intervention, identify a manifest theme and implication that bridges the surface and a latent meaning in light of the intervention context. State the decoded, underlying raw message so derived. Identify the mechanisms that transformed the latent content into the manifest-content element.

Answers:

There are many possible interventions from a therapist that could have evoked this response. A therapist could have offered a sound interpretation, could have behaved in deviant fashion (for example, if he had been sipping a bit of alcohol during the session), or could have remained appropriately silent. For this reason, we will now consider three specific possible interventions that might have evoked this particular manifest image. The reader can compare the analysis of these interventions with his or her own proposals.

For each of the interventions to be offered here, the reader should answer the questions proposed above. In addition, respond to the following:

1. If this association was a response to a sound interpretation, which surface themes would be selected to arrive at the latent meanings in this message?

2. If the patient had been on the couch and had indeed heard the therapist sipping a bit of alcohol as he sat behind her, how would you decode this manifest message?

3. If the patient had generated a flood of pressured associations, but without meaning that could be organized in light of an adaptive context, and the therapist had remained appropriately silent, which themes would then be used in decoding this particular message?

In carrying out each of these exercises, be certain to generate an unconscious, raw (decoded) image. Approach the identification of the pertinent themes by evaluating the implications of each of the proposed interventions alluded to here.

Answers:

1. A sound intervention is a form of appropriate nurturing by the therapist to the patient. This would lead to a selection of the following themes:

a. The drinking implies taking in a meaningful comment from the therapist.

b. The glass proposes that the intervention itself served as a sound container and implies the presentation of a single comment.

c. The water represents the nurturing and relief-giving quality of the intervention.

The underlying, decoded raw message could be stated as follows: I (the patient) have taken in a relief-giving intervention (from the therapist).

In terms of mechanisms, there is a displacement from the therapeutic relationship to the setting in which the drinking of the water took place. There is also symbolization, in that an intervention by the therapist is represented as a glass of water, and the patient's listening is symbolized by the incorporative drinking process.

2. There are many implications to the second adaptive context, most of them involving a pathologically destructive, self-gratifying, inappropriate act by the therapist. This particular derivative (manifest) image is therefore highly defensive and simply characterizes through displacement (from the therapist onto the patient) the concrete incorporation of a liquid, with the disguise being applied to the alcohol, which is being represented as water. The effort here is to deny and detoxify the serious implications of the therapist's alcohol intake. Thus, the underlying raw message contained in this manifest image is to the following effect: The therapist has drunk a glass of liquid. This type of defensive raw message is itself a highly disguised encoded message with few clues as to the true underlying message related to the alcohol intake. In all, this particular adaptive context reveals a rather concrete use of drinking and a glass and a defensive representation of alcohol by water.

3. In light of the adaptive context of the therapist's silence and the patient's excessive verbiage, the self-reference is a displacement from the therapist to the patient—that is, the therapist's incorporative listening is portrayed by the patient's having taken a drink. Here the drinking symbolizes listening, the glass touches on the capacity for containment by the therapist, and the water represents the patient's associations. The underlying raw message may be stated as follows: You (the therapist) have taken in the flow of my associations. This is a relatively innocuous, perceptive (i.e., nondistorted) encoded message.

DECODING MATERIAL: EXERCISE 5.2

We turn now to a second image that could have been stimulated by several different adaptive contexts. It will provide us with a further opportunity to identify themes and to understand the selection and transposing processes that take place in light of the implications of a therapist's interventions. Here, too, we have a brief excerpt from a session with a woman patient being seen by a male therapist:

> *Patient*: Someone was trapped in a flooded basement trying desperately to get out.

Respond to the following questions:

1. Take each element in this message and identify the concrete and abstract themes so contained.

2. For purposes of speculation, propose as many interventions as possible that could stimulate—that is, fit in with—this association. Remember that there is an intimate relationship between the implications of an adaptive context and a responsive derivative message. In light of this interplay, propose interventions whose implications could be encoded in the themes contained in this derivative expression. In an effort to generate an exercise for which answers can be provided, the reader is advised to consider each of the basic ground rules of psychotherapy. Attempt to transpose manifest into latent themes in light of an intervention by means of which the therapist adhered to the particular ground rule, and then carry out a comparable exercise based on the thesis that the therapist had deviated from that ground rule. In each instance, select and shape a theme from the manifest material in order to transpose and bridge it to the latent context, thereby generating a specific, decoded raw message.

Answers:

1. The following are the themes that are most evident in this segment of material:

a. "Someone" could refer to an individual who is poorly identified, as well as to a specific person—man or woman, adult or child.

b. "Trapped" could literally allude to being incarcerated or could touch on the broader themes of endangerment, restriction, detainment, imprisonment, suffocation, and perhaps being stalked or hounded.

c. "Flooded" could literally allude to to an overflow of water, such as from a tub, river, sewer, and so forth. More abstractly, "flooded" could imply being overwhelmed, bombarded, swept away, inundated, faced with a variety of excesses, having difficulties managing, being in a situation that is out of control, being under pressure, and perhaps even being smothered or suffocated. These meanings could be entirely symbolic and emotional-mental and/or physical.

d. "Basement" may again allude concretely to a variety of basement structures, as in houses, apartment houses, office buildings, and the like. More abstractly, it may stand for any subterranean place, cavern, something underground, something hidden, something below something else, a closed space, a container, a place of danger, a relatively unstructured setting, and a place with restricted egress.

e. "Trying desperately to get out," in addition to its concrete meaning, may imply escape, struggle, desperation and despair, flight, avoidance, and in general, departure from any enclosed space.

All of these images may imply some type of mental-emotional meaning, but may as well allude to physical places and the human body. To summarize, the main themes on the surface involve someone who is trapped in an inundated enclosure who wishes to escape. Emphasis has therefore been placed on images of entrapment, being overwhelmed, an enclosed space or claustrum, and the wish to extricate oneself.

2. We will turn now to each of the ground rules of psychotherapy and transpose the thematic material in light of the therapist's postulated adherence to or deviation from each of these tenets (the

adaptive context). In reviewing these answers, if the reader has not attempted to formulate this segment of associations in light of a particular ground rule (intervention context), he or she is advised to do so before reviewing the answer offered here.

a. *Set fee.* With respect to the fee, the intervention most likely to have stimulated these associations is a sudden increase. Had this occurred, these associations would reflect the patient's sense of entrapment as created by the deviation, and a view of the therapist as out of control, trying desperately to get rid of or evoking a flight response in the patient. It would be the excessive quality of the therapist act that has been represented by the flooding. The raw message would be: You (the therapist) have unilaterally increased my fee, leaving me (the patient) to feel entrapped in the presence of someone out of control. You seem to want to get rid of me, and in any case, I myself would like to escape.

Had the patient requested a reduction in fee and the therapist maintained the fee structure, the patient would then feel entrapped in an enclosure—here, the well-maintained therapeutic situation. The flooding would more likely represent a reactive response in the patient (a fear of losing control), as would the thought of getting out of the situation.

On the other hand, if the fee had been reduced by the therapist, the sense of entrapment would involve the seductive aspects of the intervention and, once again, a view of the therapist out of control, attempting to push the patient out of treatment. Even more likely, the patient would be thinking of leaving therapy because of the seductive danger.

In general, maintaining the ground rules of psychotherapy creates a claustrum that is unconsciously viewed, only partly because of distortion, as entrapping and creating dangers of losing control—on the part of the patient, the therapist, or both. Alterations in the ground rules tend to produce images of the therapist as a person who feels trapped in the therapeutic claustrum and is out of control; he or she is viewed as attempting to escape the danger situation by way of the modification in the ground rule. This particular type of imagery, then, is rather typical when alterations have occurred in the ground rules of psychotherapy; in general, however, even though the patient feels endangered, if the therapist maintains the frame, there is a sense of basic trust and security so that there is little unconscious wish to take flight. (This, although the conscious expression may, to the contrary, express such a desire.)

b. *Set length of sessions.* If the therapist had shortened a session, this material would readily reflect an encoded view of the therapist as someone who felt entrapped and overwhelmed (flooded) during the session and therefore dismissed the patient—sent her out—prematurely. If the patient herself had left the hour early, the image would apply mainly to her. On the other hand, if the therapist had inadvertently *extended* the hour, it would mainly be the patient who had perceived herself as entrapped by the therapist, who had lost control; there would then be a reactive wish to escape his entrapment.

Of all the ground rule interventions, an alteration in the set length of sessions is high among the deviations most likely to produce this particular segment of associations. Had the patient requested a shortening or extension of her hour and the therapist maintained the frame, the imagery would apply to the patient herself. In contrast, if the therapist had acceded to such a request, the main images would apply to the therapist (and only secondarily to the patient).

c. *Set frequency of sessions.* Here, a similar principle to the one developed regarding the length of the hour would apply, but less forcefully. If the therapist had decreased the frequency of sessions, the patient would perceive him as flooded and trapped by the regular schedule and as needing to escape the dangerous claustrum by decreasing the frequency of hours. If the frequency had been increased, the patient might perceive both herself and the therapist as trapped in a more intense treatment situation and wish to escape.

d. If the therapist had recommended the couch to the patient, and the patient had acceded, this material could represent the patient's experience of entrapment and wish to escape. If the therapist had advised the patient to sit up rather than lie on the couch, this segment would reflect the therapist's own fears of entrapment and his need to help the patient get out of the entrapping situation.

e. If the therapist had invoked the fundamental rule of free association, and the patient was especially anxious about this, the image would reflect her own sense of entrapment, as well as fears of being flooded by the therapist's interventions or of flooding him with her material. It would also include a responsive wish to escape from treatment. If the intervention involved the therapist excusing the patient from the fundamental rule of free association, it would reflect the therapist's own fear of entrapment by the patient's flooded associations, and his extricating himself from this danger by modifying this particular tenet.

f. If the therapist had maintained his sense of anonymity, it is unlikely that this image would have been generated. On the other hand, if the therapist had engaged in self-revelations and expressions of personal opinions, these noninterpretive interventions could be perceived by the patient as excessive (the flooding), entrapping, an escape by the therapist from his responsibilities to hold the frame and interpret, an act of desperation, and could have evoked wishes within the patient to leave treatment.

g. If the therapist had maintained the one-to-one relationship in face of pressures from the patient to introduce a third party to therapy, the patient may well have felt anxious and trapped and entertained fantasies of escape. On the other hand, had the therapist introduced an outsider into the therapy, the sequence would reflect an encoded image of the therapist's fear of entrapment and his need to escape by introducing another person into the treatment situation.

h. As for total confidentiality, adhering to this tenet would lead the patient to feel entrapped and desperate to leave, whereas modifying this tenet would reflect a flight by the therapist from his fears of incarceration with the patient.

i. With respect to the use of neutral interventions, a valid intervention might lead the patient to feel somewhat entrapped and to wish to escape treatment because of the sense of power evident in the therapist, although such anxieties are usually secondary and not the main response to sound therapeutic work. On the other hand, an erroneous intervention, especially one that is not interpretive, is commonly perceived as flooding the patient with the therapist's own words and needs, and as entrapping, and usually evokes wishes for escape.

It can be seen, then, that many deviations and errant interventions evoke themes shared in common—that is, convey common universal meanings. In addition, each deviation will generate specific meanings and images in keeping with its particular nature and function. The specific latent content in a given message depends mainly on the nature of the deviation, the state of the therapeutic interaction, and the patient's own pathologically determined selective responses.

To complete this exercise, we may consider more carefully the influence of the two adaptive contexts constituting interventions that could have most likely evoked this particular sequence of images: the shortening of the patient's session and its extension. With respect to the former adaptive context, as noted, the "someone" who is trapped in the session is the therapist, who has a need to send the patient out of the hour prematurely in order to escape his sense of entrapment. The basement is a displaced representation of the therapy consultation room. There is a sense that the therapist has been overwhelmed (flooded) by something in the patient's material, and through an error committed in desperation, arranges to escape. Here the symbols are someone, being trapped, being flooded, the basement, and trying to get out. Each represents an aspect of the following encoded raw message: You (the therapist) felt trapped in the consultation room alone with me (the patient), flooded by my material and unconscious communications (the basement), and desperately anxious; you found it necessary to escape by dismissing me early. It is this transposed raw message that is embodied in the story of the individual trapped in the flooded basement, trying desperately to get out.

If the adaptive context was the extension of the patient's hour, then the someone who is trapped is primarily the patient herself. It is she who is flooded or overwhelmed by the therapist's own incapacity to manage the situation, and she views the therapist as flooded as well. The basement is both the consultation office and the unconscious communications that have disturbed the therapist. Because the therapist is entrapping the patient, it is mainly the patient who wishes desperately to get out.

It is important to recognize the principle that encoded images that are in keeping with the implications of an adaptive context are defined as *unconscious perceptions*. Their main designation involves a valid encoded image of the therapist. Through condensation, however, the same material may contain a reliable encoded image of the patient him or herself.

In addition, those images which are *not* in keeping with the nature of an adaptive context must be viewed as *reactions to perceptions*. In the example of the extended hour, the patient reacts to the therapist's entrapping interventions with wishes to escape. Other common reactions to perceptions of intervention contexts include efforts to help or cure the therapist, to offer encoded perspectives and interpretations, to propose models of correction or rectification, wishes and efforts to harm the therapist, and evocative conscious and unconscious fantasies and memories.

In principle, then, a series of manifest images presented in one context (here, the flooding of a basement) generates a series of concrete and abstract meanings that can then be applied to a second situation (here, the treatment experience, and a particular intervention from the therapist). It is critical to develop a sense of how bridging and transposed themes are portrayed in the material from patients—narratives and images that express one meaning on the surface and another unconsciously. This is the heart of the encoding and decoding processes.

DECODING MATERIAL: EXERCISE 5.3

The following extract pertains to a young woman patient in psychotherapy with a male therapist for episodes of depression. In the prior session, the therapist had announced that he had decided to give up his private practice in favor of a full-time position he was to assume at a somewhat distant clinic.

The next session began as follows:

> *Patient*: For some reason, I've been thinking about how my mother sometimes wouldn't talk to me. I'd feel abandoned. My boyfriend, as you know, is an internist. Sometimes he gets so preoccupied with his own problems, he neglects his patients. I think he should be more responsible and committed to his work. This week he felt overwhelmed by his practice and withdrew. Now he plans to take a vacation next week. I don't trust his attitude. When I was a child and my parents would go away, I'd begin to wheeze. I wheezed a little yesterday, but I don't know why. I'm having fantasies of letting my boyfriend impregnate me.

Respond to the following questions:

1. Name the main adaptive context (stimulus) for this material.

2. What are the most notable implications of this intervention context?

3. Sentence by sentence, identify the concrete and abstract themes contained in these associations. If there are other additional themes represented by the sequence of sentences, identify them as well.

4. For each sentence, use the adaptive context to decode its unconscious meaning. In so doing, first, identify the key themes that bridge the manifest content and the latent content, and then translate the manifest narrative into a decoded raw message.

Answers:

1. The key adaptive context is the therapist's decision to leave his practice and to terminate with the patient.

2. This decision is a major violation of an implied aspect of the ground rules of psychotherapy: that the therapist will be available to the patient until the patient has resolved his or her madness (presenting and unfolding emotional difficulties). The intervention creates an image of the therapist that the patient is likely to mistrust and which will disturb her sense of reality testing—a long-standing and realistic expectation has been shattered. The therapist will also be seen as parasitizing the patient, as shifting to action-discharge rather than maintaining the pursuit of understanding, as disturbing the communicative relationship between himself and the patient, and especially as selfishly abandoning the patient based on his own personal (pathological) needs—needs that disregard the therapeutic requirements of the patient. The experience may also have overtones of violence and of a sexually assaultive act, and separation

issues will be accentuated. There is a sense that the therapist is using the patient narcissistically as a selfobject, and that he himself is struggling with an identity disturbance. For the patient, the intervention will be seen as an act of madness.

In sum, the main attributes of this intervention involve the violation of an implicit pledge to the patient, the self-centered qualities of the decision, and the sense of violence and abandonment. In attempting to decipher each of the patient's messages in the session presented above, we will use these attributes as our decoding keys. In addition, we should be mindful of the likelihood that the patient will encode additional dimensions of this intervention that have been overlooked in these initial anticipatory formulations.

3. The following are the main concrete and abstract themes contained in each communicative segment in this material:

a. In alluding to the patient's mother not talking to her and her feeling of abandonment, the patient has introduced manifest themes related to her mother and, more abstractly, maternal and all types of caring. There is a theme of not talking, which may touch upon more abstract themes such as noncommunication, abandonment, absence, the punitive use of silence, being oppositional, and all forms of deprivation. In feeling abandoned, there is the concrete theme of desertion, as well as the broader themes of loss, being alone, hostile deprivation, absence, and flight.

It will soon be necessary to select from these themes those that fit best with the latent raw image—those that are relevant to the adaptive context of the therapist's intervention.

b. The next sentence involves the boyfriend's role as a doctor and his becoming preoccupied with his own problems to the neglect of his patients. There are themes of physician (the therapist was a psychiatrist) and, more abstractly, caring and healing individuals, being a professional, medicine, and medical responsibilities. The next part of this sentence alludes to preoccupation, distraction, self-absorption, withdrawal (note the repetition of this particular theme—often a sign of an important latent theme), loss of interest, autism, noncommunication, loss in general, and rumination. There is also an allusion to having problems suggestive of emotional difficulties and even of psychopathology. Finally, there is neglect of patients, which again brings up images of abandonment and lack of care, as well as the theme of patients, those in need, those in a subservient position, those depending on others, and the like.

In these first two communicative segments, the themes of autistic withdrawal, abandonment, neglect, and selfishness loom large. The repetition of such themes tends to point to their importance on a latent level—that is, in light of the adaptive context. These images should have special pertinence and be an important aspect of the patient's latent raw messages and perceptions.

c. In the comment regarding the patient's belief that the boyfriend should be more responsible and committed to his work, there are themes of responsibility and commitment, involvement, sound functioning, investment in one's efforts, loyalty, and devotion.

These themes are connected to the boyfriend's work, an allusion once again to his functioning as a physician; this comment once again represents this particular theme.

d. In alluding to the boyfriend being overwhelmed by his practice and withdrawing, the patient touches on themes of being overwhelmed, medical work, and withdrawal. More abstract are themes of inundation, not being able to function, being unable to cope, being flooded, being overburdened, and failing to deal adequately with a particular situation. The reference to the medical practice again touches upon the theme of medical work. The withdrawal is once again a theme related to desertion, abandonment, and such.

e. Next the patient mentions that the boyfriend is taking a vacation next week. This comment alludes to vacation, absence, being left, separation, not working, resting or traveling, and leaving others. The mention of the following week touches on the consideration of future events.

f. In the patient's comment about not trusting her boyfriend's attitude, there is the evident theme of mistrust, as well as wariness, uncertainty, concern, a sense of unreliability, and suspiciousness.

g. In the comment regarding her parents' leaving and her response with wheezing, we have again the theme of abandonment and being left, with all of its attendant meanings. The wheezing refers specifically to an asthmatic-like symptom, trouble breathing, problems taking in or incorporating, and physical illness.

h. In stating that the patient wheezed a little yesterday and that she is uncertain why, the themes related to wheezing are repeated. There is also an allusion to time past and to being uncertain, not understanding, and the like.

i. In the final sentence regarding having the boyfriend impregnate her, we have the themes of fantasy, imagination, and daydream. There is also the allusion again to the boyfriend, bringing up themes of men, friendship, lover, commitment, and social involvement. Finally, the image of being impregnated brings up pregnancy, sexual intercourse, the act of impregnation, being entered, fusion and merger, containing a fetus, nurturing, and such—all in a context that suggests an out-of-wedlock impregnation and, therefore, the violation of certain social boundaries and mores.

It is evident that this is a sequence of associations rich in narrative and imagery and therefore rich in thematic content. The main themes involve abandonment, selfish withdrawal, being overwhelmed, the need to be more responsible, a physical symptomatic response to separation, and impregnation. As yet, we have not developed a sense of which of these themes are best characterized as aspects of valid encoded perceptions of the therapist in light of the intervention context, and which involve responses to these perceptions—mainly in the form of models of rectification and fantasy-memory formations. As noted, the former will be based on images that are in keeping with the known implications of the adaptive context, whereas the latter would not fit with such meanings. In developing transposed, decoded, raw latent messages, the distinction between perception and response to perception should be clearly stated.

4. The following appears to be the best available decoding efforts as applied to this material. We will attempt now to characterize the raw latent messages contained in these communicative elements, transposing manifest themes in light of the adaptive contexts in which they will be placed as latent raw images—the stimulus or trigger being the therapist's decision to abandon his practice and terminate the patient.

a. The allusion to the mother not talking to the patient and the patient's feeling abandoned appears to be an encoded perception of the therapist in light of his intervention. The main bridging (transposable) themes would involve abstracting the mother's not talking to the patient to the themes of absence, and of action or acting against (this latter meaning is added at this point in light of a known implication of the adaptive context, namely, the shift from understanding to action-discharge). Pertinent, too, is the theme of abandonment, which serves directly to bridge the manifest context (the loss of the mother) to the latent context (the loss of the therapist). Thus this first communicative element can be decoded into the following raw message in light of the adaptive context: You (the therapist), as my mother before you, have withdrawn from and abandoned me.

For purposes of transposition, we have selected the theme of withdrawal as contained in the image of someone not talking to another person. Because the adaptive context does not involve silence, but instead entails abandonment and loss, it was necessary to select an abstract theme inherent to the manifest image that would bridge from the surface to the latent (therapy-pertinent) context. Through displacement and symbolic representation, the therapist's decision to terminate the patient's treatment is represented by the patient's mother not talking to the patient. Departure is portrayed by silence. In selecting this particular symbolic representation, the patient is expressing a genetic connection between the behavior of the therapist and an earlier pathogenic behavior of the mother. Because there is on some level here an actual repetition of a past pathogenic trauma, this genetic formulation has perceptive and nontransference implications and is neither distorted nor an expression of transference.

With respect to the decoding of the manifest content into a latent raw image, we have simply taken the theme of abandonment on a manifest level and undone the use of displacement from the therapist onto the earlier situation between the patient and her mother. Abandonment fits quite well with the latent context, the therapist's intervention—his plans to terminate with the patient. There is thus both the use of symbolism and the simple use of displacement in this first encoded message. In addition, the raw message touches on important dynamic implications of the therapist's termination decision—its withdrawal and desertion attributes.

b. Next, there is the image of the physician boyfriend who gets preoccupied with his own problems and neglects his patients. Here the theme of physician is subjected to displacement, while the abandonment is now given the quality of neglect—a more irresponsible image. The boyfriend's preoccupation with his own problems is best abstracted as representing the selfish reasons, entirely personal, for which the therapist had made this decision. These three themes best characterize both the manifest and latent contents of this communicative segment. They are the transposed or bridging themes.

The resultant raw message may be stated as follows: You are a physician and yet you selfishly worry about your own problems rather than those of your patients; you are therefore quite neglectful of them—including me. Here there is an implied stress on physicianly responsibility, the pathological narcissistic and self-serving aspects of a therapist's decision and its neglectful quality. These are all compelling encoded perceptions of implications of the adaptive context. There is as yet no major reaction to these perceptions, though the image of the patient's feeling abandoned contains both an encoded perception of the therapist's desertion and her reactive sense of loss.

c. The patient's comment that the boyfriend should be more responsible and committed to his work appears to be an encoded *corrective* or *model of rectification* addressed to the therapist through displacement onto the physician-friend. In light of the adaptive context of the therapist's decision to terminate his patients and his practice, this communicative segment cannot be viewed as an encoded perception—it does not characterize an implication of this particular effort. Indeed, the adaptive context speaks more of irresponsibility and lack of commitment than the reverse. It is this absence of fit with the implications of an intervention context that leads one to formulate the patient's message as a reaction to a direct or encoded perception of the therapist. Here, the patient is holding up a model to the therapist. The underlying raw message can be stated as follows: You (the therapist) should be more responsible to your work and to your patients; you should not suddenly abandon them.

d. The next communicative sequence involves the physician-boyfriend being overwhelmed by his practice and then withdrawing, and his decision to take a vacation the following week. Here again there are themes which touch on valid perceptions mixed with a reasonable measure of speculation. The patient perceives or suspects that the therapist feels overwhelmed by his work, that he is withdrawing, and that on this basis, he has decided to leave his practice. The theme of vacation must be abstracted and generalized to the theme of leaving, and then specifically attached to the latent adaptive context to generate the raw message of a therapist deserting one's patients. It is notable that the patient portrays a permanent departure of the therapist through a vacation by the boyfriend, the latter implying the return of the individual who has left. This particular choice of symbolic representation, then, embodies a wish within the patient that the therapist's departure be a temporary one. Thus, although the choice of these representations seems determined mainly by the nature of the adaptive context (and secondarily by the patient's own genetic and separation sensitivities), a further factor in the choice of symbols has emerged: their use to represent wishes and needs within the patient.

The image of the therapist as being overwhelmed is a mixture of perception and fantasy, though, in the main, it is a characterization of a likely dimension of the therapist's decision. The underlying raw message can be stated as follows: You (the therapist) seem to be overwhelmed by me and your other patients and by doing psychotherapy. As a result, you have decided to leave us. I wish you were returning.

e. The comment regarding the mistrust of the doctor-boyfriend reflects the patient's perception of the untrustworthiness of the therapist who closes his practice. At the same time, it characterizes a reaction within the patient. Displacement has been the main vehicle of transposition. It involves a shift from the therapist onto the boyfriend. The underlying raw message is: You (the therapist) cannot be trusted because of your decision to terminate my therapy.

f. The next communicative segment involves the patient's wheezing when her parents left and her wheezing on the day prior to the session. The parents' leaving is an encoded representation of the therapist's decision to terminate the patient's therapy, a representation that involves mainly the use of displacement—here, from the therapist onto the patient's parents. Simultaneously, the image represents a minimally disguised (symbolized) genetic connection linking the therapist's departure with experiences involving the patient's parents. Here, too, the basic configuration is nontransferential in nature, in that the therapist is in reality repeating a pathogenic trauma created by the patient's parents in her childhood.

The wheezing may be viewed as a psychosomatic symptom that in itself does not reveal its own unconscious meanings. Rather than attempting to decode such an image, we are more likely to describe its qualities or suggest inferences. In the main, the wheezing is a pathological psychosomatic form of madness that in all likelihood reflects unconscious meanings encoded in the balance of the excerpt. It appears to be a response to the patient's view of the therapist as abandoning her, as being overwhelmed, and as responding selfishly to his own problems instead of her therapeutic needs. The proposals that the wheezing represents a difficulty in breathing, a sense of suffocation, a cry for help, although tentative and possible, are either simple inferences or the fantasy-products of the therapist. Although such speculations have their place in psychotherapy, they must eventually be validated by the decoding process as evidence that they are indeed the patient's intended meanings.

The patient's report that she had wheezed on the day prior to the session also does not lend itself to decoding. Instead, it suggests an important inference: because wheezing is a response in the patient to separation, it has emerged at this time as a reaction to the therapist's planned departure. Again, this inference must be validated by decoding other material that does indeed contain derivative meaning.

As for the underlying raw message, all that can be stated is: You (the therapist) are leaving me as my parents did in the past. In each instance, I responded with wheezing.

g. The patient's fantasy of impregnation by the boyfriend appears to be a displaced wish directed toward the therapist. It may involve a desire to be united with the therapist or the concrete wish for his child. These are images that, once again, do not fit with the implications of the prevailing adaptive context, and which therefore must be formulated as a response to the perception of the therapist's abandonment. Longings of this type are not uncommon as a reaction to separation and loss; they require interpretation lest the patient unwittingly (and unconsciously) act out the fantasy-wish. The raw encoded message appears to be: I (the patient) wish to undo the anticipation of your loss [a part of the raw message derived from the patient's other associations] by being united with you in some emotional-physical way, by having your baby, or both.

CONCLUDING COMMENTS

This completes our study of the essentials of the decoding process in psychotherapy. The patient's associations in a psychotherapy session move along at a rather fast pace. As a result, the therapist must move continuously back and forth between realizations related to the implications of the prevailing adaptive contexts and the manifest imagery of the patient. Each surface image is quickly lifted from its manifest context and placed into (transposed into) a context related to one or another implication of the intervention context. At bottom, then, this critical effort requires a considerable degree of self-knowledge and a comprehensive understanding of the nature and function of each intervention made by a psychotherapist.

Although difficult, the proper use of the decoding process is quite rewarding for patient and therapist alike. It is an art that requires study, practice, and the resolution of major countertransference problems as well. Still, it is a skill that can be applied with great empathy and atunement to the patient's unconscious needs and communications, and with due respect for surface expressions. It is an ability well worth mastering, because the decoding of derivative messages is the only road to the unconscious foundation of the patient's madness (and secondarily, of the therapist's madness as well).

Notes

6 The Absence of Encoded Meaning

In general, psychotherapists are committed to a search for meaning in the material from patients by way of understanding and insight. This can create a prejudice, however, that renders the therapist likely to find meaning in *all* of the patient's associations. When it comes specifically to the presence of encoded meaning in a patient's productions, studies have shown considerable variability in patient expressions. At one extreme are those encoded communications that are fraught with multiple meanings and decodable in light of pertinent adaptive contexts. At the other extreme lie communicative segments without notable decipherable implications, flat and empty in light of all known intervention contexts.

THE ABSENCE OF MEANING: EXERCISE 6.1

The excerpt that follows pertains to a young man who sought psychotherapy because of suicidal fantasies and impulses. He was seen in a clinic by a male therapist who had become frustrated with his patient's many questions in a session that took place some three months into the therapy. The therapist had confronted the patient with his demands and had noted the hostile qualities of his pressures. And yet, the therapist proceeded to attempt to answer in detail the patient's many queries about the clinic, the nature of psychotherapy, his impressions of the patient, and the like. The patient then missed the next session. The following dialogue ensued at the beginning of the next hour.

> *Patient*: This guy I live with, he got me into a fight. We wrestled and he banged my head against a chair. I've nothing more to say. I feel angry. Aren't you going to talk? You talked a lot last time.
>
> *Therapist*: You seem agitated today and displeased with the therapy.
>
> *Patient*: I want to know how therapy is supposed to work. I need some answers. I know I'm an angry guy. Where do I get all that aggression from? Is it in that thing called the id? Is it in my mind or my body? I want you to talk. I read that hostility comes from frustration. I had this fantasy of meeting you in a bar or somewhere, and having a drink with you. Buddy-buddy, I guess. Why do I get so dependent on people?

Answer the following questions in regard to the above material:

1. Name the two adaptive contexts in this material, paying attention to both the introduction and the excerpt from the hour. Identify the main attributes of each of these contexts.

2. Identify the themes in each communicative segment of the patient's material, separating the associations that appeared before the therapist's intervention from those that appeared after it. Can you give these themes latent meaning in light of the preceding adaptive context? If so, state the underlying raw message. If not, identify those segments of material which appear to lack derivative qualities and are therefore without notable derivative (unconscious) meaning.

Answers:

1. The first adaptive context appears in the introduction to the hour and is constituted by the therapist's confrontation of the patient in regard to his demandingness and hostility and, in addition, his direct answers to the patient's questions.

The second adaptive context is the therapist's intervention in the excerpted hour, to the effect that the patient appears agitated today and displeased with the therapy.

As for implications, the first intervention is nonneutral and a subtle modification of the ideal ground rules of therapy. It has qualities of the autistic and parasitic modes of relatedness in that it fails to understand and attacks the patient. It also suggests an action-discharge mode of cure in that it lacks an effort directed toward insight and appears to be serving as a discharge mechanism for the therapist—even though it is confined to the verbal-affective sphere. Communication is fixed on the manifest-content level, and nonderivative expression is encouraged from the patient. Also, the harshness of the therapist's intervention might well interfere with the openness of communication between patient and therapist.

There is a clearly hostile and defensive quality to these interventions, which might also have attributes of homosexual penetration. There is a reflection, too, of a loss of clear identity in the therapist and signs of narcissistic rage. The interventions have qualities of madness. In the main, then, the first set of interventions are noninterpretive and uninsightful, a form of action-discharge and parasiticism of the patient, with strikingly hostile and likely latent homosexual qualities.

The second intervention is an attempt at confrontation and a general interpretation. It does not significantly impinge upon the framework of the psychotherapy, though it has autistic qualities in its lack of understanding of the patient (a loss of the meaning link between therapist and patient). Thus, no attention was paid to the derivative communications in the hour as they illuminate the patient's perceptions of the therapist in light of his interventions of the previous session. Communication is focused on a manifest level with a full measure of inference. On the whole, this is a relatively nondescript manifest-content confrontation, whose main function is to avoid the patient's unconscious perceptions of the attributes of the therapist's interventions in the previous session. As such, it has a powerful defensive quality and could well stimulate strong communicative defenses in the patient.

2. If we consider now the excerpted material, the following is pertinent:

a. The first association about the "guy" who fought with the patient, banging his head against the chair, contains an allusion to a man, a roommate, someone with whom space is shared, someone with whom the patient sleeps in some sense, whether in the apartment or in the shared bed. The allusion to sharing space with another man suggests a displacement from the therapist and an encoded representation of the treatment relationship and situation.

The next part of this communicative element involves the fight, wrestling, and the head banging, and therefore themes of fight, dispute, argument, disagreement, and other comparable images, as well as hostile physical contact, a direct attack on the head, attempts to injure, and the like. The chair may be a clue to the setting, in that it may translate into a context related to the psychotherapy.

In light of the implications of the therapist's intervention of the previous hour, the following raw message may be decoded from this initial communicative segment: You (the therapist) got me into a fight much as I engaged you in a battle. I experienced your interventions as part of a wrestling match and found your confrontations and direct answers to my questions an assault on my head. This encoded perception is the result of a selection process determined in part by the patient's own latent homosexuality and hostility, although it also portrays accurately selected unconscious implications of the therapist's previous interventions.

In regard to the next communicative section, the patient first states that he has nothing more to say—themes of emptiness, not wanting to talk, not knowing what to say, wanting to bring treatment to a halt, and the like. Based on the patient's healthy and universal *unconscious* expectation of an interpretive intervention from the therapist, this particular segment may be decoded as follows: In your (the therapist's) intervention, you revealed that you have nothing meaningful to say to me. In response, I no longer wish to talk to you. In any case, your clinging to the surface has deprived our interaction of unconscious meaning.

Next, the patient's feeling of anger may reflect a displaced perception (from the therapist onto the patient himself) of the hostility contained in the therapist's confrontations and direct responses to the patient's questions.

The next segment, in which the patient asks the therapist if he is going to talk, contains allusions to speaking, but seems especially thin as a potential derivative expression. It is possible to decode this segment in the following manner: Last session you (the therapist) did not talk meaningfully; in this hour, I am beginning to lose my wish to talk meaningfully to you in return. It appears, however, that the patient is beginning to approach the use of relatively nonderivative expressions.

The comment that the therapist talked a lot last time is a direct allusion to his previous interventions. While the themes of talking, speaking aloud, and last session, do arise, they appear to have little in the way of derivative quality. It is not uncommon for manifest allusions to therapy and to the therapist to lack encoded valences—that is, they tend to be quite direct and single-message expressions.

b. If we consider now the material that followed the therapist's intervention in the session, the patient's comment that he wants to know how therapy is supposed to work contains themes of wanting knowledge, an allusion to therapy, and concerns with how it works. While there may be an encoded implication that the therapist, in light of his nonadaptive-context intervention, does not know how therapy is supposed to work, this meaning is quite thin. At best, this particular element is marginal with respect to derivative meaning.

Next the patient states he needs some answers, an element that contains an allusion to need and answers. While there is an implication that the patient is not getting his needs met and that he is not obtaining an understanding of the unconscious basis of his madness, this element also appears to be relatively nonderivative in nature.

Next the patient states that he knows he is "an angry guy." While the prior intervention lacks an understanding of the patient, it is not especially hostile. Thus the allusion to anger does not appear to be an encoded perception of the therapist (of course it may well be a perception based on the therapist's intervention in the previous session), although the anger may apply to the patient as stated. In the segment itself there is the theme of knowing, understanding, anger, and sexual identity—being a guy. In all, we have here another element with little in the way of encoded meaning—none of these themes are readily transposed and given meaning in light of prevailing adaptive contexts.

Next the patient asks where he gets his aggression from, a question about sources and aggression, although it embodies little in the way of encoded meaning. This is characteristic of most intellectualized associations. There then follows the allusion to the id, another intellectualized statement that seems to have little in the way of derivative valence. Similarly, the next segment has to do with themes of mind and body, all of it manifest, with little encoded meaning in light of the prior intervention. Also, the patient's request that the therapist talk seems manifest, with little encoded implication. There is little or no evidence of the patient's use of displacement and symbolization.

There follows the patient's mention that he read that hostility comes from frustration, a further intellectualized segment that deals with sources, hostility, frustration, and little else. We then have the patient's *conscious* fantasy of meeting the therapist in a bar somewhere and having a drink with him, buddy-buddy. This particular manifest fantasy has to do with meeting someone in a bar, having a drink, taking something in, being friendly, and perhaps some allusion to implied homosexuality. As such, it contains little in the way of derivative response to the therapist's interventions in the present hour. It does, however, touch upon, in encoded fashion, some of the unconscious attributes of the therapist's interventions in the previous session—their latent homosexual meanings and their nontherapeutic quality; answering questions is an acceptable social response rather than an appropriate (valid) response from a psychotherapist.

Finally, the patient's question as to why he is so dependent on people is an intellectualized allusion to dependency and others, with little in the way of encoded meaning.

In sum, then, the segment that follows the therapist's intervention in the hour contains many single-message nonderivative associations. This determination was made by attempting to identify the themes contained in each communicative element, and further, ascertaining whether they lend themselves to transposition by fitting in with (bridging over to) implications of the prevailing adaptive contexts. These associations illustrate well the type of material that is often communicated in linear, nonderivative fashion: direct allusions to the therapist, intellectualizations, speculations, readings, and self-interpretations. In addition, emotional and physical symptoms tend to be poor carriers of derivative meaning, as are thin derivative elements with self-evident meanings or implications. In general, when material of this kind appears in a patient's associations, the existence of multiple-message, decodable derivatives is unlikely. Again, it is well to realize that the unconscious encoding process involves displacement and disguise—in the main, the modification of raw perceptions of the therapist (and reactive responses) in light of disturbing or valid interventions. Since the latent raw messages involve the therapist, the therapist and therapeutic situation will virtually always be subjected to displacement and disguise if unconscious meaning is intended. Because of this, direct allusions to the therapist and to the treatment experience are likely to be linear and lack encoded valence. At times, of course, a patient may utilize an allusion to one aspect of treatment in order to encode a different aspect. However, the use of displacement is minimal under such circumstances, and the risk of ready detection of the latent raw message great. In general, the most cogent displacement involves a shift from the therapist to the patient, because therapists are least likely to realize that self-addressed comments and images conveyed by their patients may contain encoded images of themselves—the therapists. As noted before, the absence of narratives and imagery tends to signal single-message communication and a relative absence of derivative expression.

SOME FINAL PERSPECTIVES

This completes our study of the encoding and decoding processes in psychotherapy in terms of its most fundamental aspects. Volume II in this series (Langs, in press) will take up where the present book closes: it will be concerned with the specific structure of the patient's associations in the psychotherapy session, the definitive decoding of the patient's material, and the listening process of the therapist that leads to integrated interventions. Through the present work, it is hoped that the reader has been able to develop a sense of the importance of unconscious communication as it pertains to the basic nature of madness and psychopathology—and as it presents a specific challenge to the therapist who wishes to work insightfully with patients. To do so, it is essential to decode unconscious messages. This is the way that one derives an understanding of the underlying foundation of psychopathology.

Far more than a lost art, decoding efforts are an art waiting to be discovered. For too long now, psychoanalysts and psychotherapists have eschewed such efforts in favor of work with manifest-content material and inference making. There are clearly understandable defensive reasons for such an approach, in that derivative expressions are indeed the royal road to the experience of madness. In consequence, both patients and therapists have sought after derivative expressions only ambivalently and heavily defended themselves against them when they actually threaten to emerge.

In concluding, then, it is well to be reminded that the therapist who is capable of decoding the material from patients embarks upon a serious and anxiety-provoking search for expressions of madness and its ultimate meaning. Such a quest is fraught with danger for both participants to treatment; nonetheless, its success offers both patient and therapist alike unique opportunities for mastery and adaptation. It is a search well worth the effort and well worth the pain.

Notes

APPENDIX

The Seven Dimensions of the Therapeutic Interaction

I. The Ground Rules, or Frame

A. *The secure frame*—offers basic trust, clear interpersonal boundaries, support for reality testing, sound holding and containment. Sources of anxiety: responsibility and confinement that produces claustrophobic anxieties, fears of losing control—of unbridled sexuality, aggression, including fantasied rage toward the therapist, and dread of annihilation by the therapist.

B. *The deviant frame*—offers basic mistrust, impaired interpersonal boundaries, disturbances in reality testing. Sources of inappropriate gratification: serves as a basis for pathological defense via merger, offers counterphobic and manic-fusion defenses, and the escape from experienced subjective madness.

C. Other implications center on the nature of the specific deviation, the moment at which an aspect of the frame is secured, ramifications of the ongoing therapeutic interaction, and the specific meanings for both patient and therapist.

II. The Mode of Relatedness

A. *Healthy symbiosis*—for the patient, accepting the conditions of treatment, free associating, attending to the therapist's interventions, and being prepared to analyze all proposed deviations from the ideal frame. For the therapist, securing the frame and adopting a basic interpretive-reconstructive stance.

B. *Pathological symbiosis*—for the patient, the search for or achievement of frame breaks and noninterpretive interventions that are inappropriately gratifying. For the therapist, the offer of such interventions, as well as obtaining inappropriate satisfactions from the patient beyond the fee and evidence of the patient's improvement.

C. *Healthy autism*—for the patient, expressions of nonmeaning at a time when there is no pressing adaptive context to which to respond. For the therapist, silence in response to material that is without meaning and therefore requires no intervention.

D. *Pathological autism*—for the patient, the absence of meaning in the face of an activated (disturbing) intervention context. For the therapist, either a failure to intervene in the presence of meaningful associational material or an intervention that does not properly construe the patient's associations, thereby introducing images and contents that derive primarily from the therapist.

E. *Pathological parasiticism*—the exploitation and harm or frustration of one participant to therapy by the other.

III. Mode of Cure

A. *True insight*—generated by interpreting an expression of the patient's madness in a given session in light of the implications of an intervention by the therapist that has activated the madness. The effort is carried out in terms of the patient's derivative complex—encoded perceptions and reactions to these perceptions, which reveal the unconscious meanings of the pathological expression.

B. *Action-discharge*—constituted by a noninterpretive intervention or any effort other than those which interpret or secure the frame, including the dumping aspects and erroneous use of verbal interventions.

C. The additional consideration as to whether the patient's material expresses basic *curative or harmful wishes* directed toward the therapist and similar consideration of the therapist's work with the patient.

IV. Mode of Communication

The degree to which derivative expressions are implicitly supported by the interventions of the therapist: the openness and freedom with which the patient is encouraged to express him or herself; considerations of communicative style (the presence of meaning or its absence): and a study of whether the patient's associations and behaviors reflect quiet communication or dumping (the use of projective identification and efforts to arouse the therapist).

V. Dynamics and Genetics

The vicissitudes of the sexual and aggressive instinctual drives; issues related to id, ego, and superego; problems of intrapsychic and interpersonal conflict and of psychosexual and aggressive development; reflections of all forms of psychodynamics; and the pertinent history of the patient and, secondarily, of the therapist.

VI. Identity and Narcissism

Implications that pertain to self-serving needs, the use of the other as a selfobject, tension regulation, ideals and values, self-esteem, and the like—for both patient and therapist.

VII. Madness and Sanity

The vicissitudes of the psychopathology of both patient and therapist.

References

Arlow, J. (1963). Conflict, regression, and symptom formation. *International Journal of Psycho-Analysis*, 44:12–22.
Bion, W. (1977). *Seven Servants*. New York: Aronson.
Freud, S. (1900). The interpretation of dreams. *Standard Edition*, 4-5:1–627.
Freud, S. (1908). Hysterical phantasies and their relationship to bisexuality. *Standard Edition*, 9:155–166.
Freud, S. (1915). Repression. *Standard Edition*, 14:141–158.
Freud, S. (1926). Inhibitions, Symptoms and Anxiety. *Standard Edition*, 20:77-178.
Gedo, J. (1979). *Beyond Interpretation*. New York: International Universities Press.
Gill, M. (1979). The analysis of the transference. *Journal of the American Psychoanalytic Association* 27 (Supplement) :263–288.
Gill, M. (1982). *Analysis of Transference: Vol. 1, Theory and Technique*. New York: International Universities Press.
Langs, R. (1978). *The Listening Process*. New York: Aronson.
Langs, R. (1981a). Modes of 'cure' in psychoanalysis and psychoanalytic psychotherapy. *International Journal of Psycho-Analysis*, 62:199–214.
Langs, R. (1981b). *Resistances and Interventions*. New York: Aronson.
Langs, R. (1982). *Psychotherapy: A Basic Text*. New York: Aronson.
Langs, R. (1983). *Unconscious Communication in Everyday Life*. New York: Aronson.
Langs, R. (in press). *A Workbook for Psychotherapists: Vol. II, Listening and Formulating*. Emerson: Newconcept Press.
Schafer, R. (1976). *A New Language for Psychoanalysis*. New Haven: Yale University Press.

Index

ABOUT THE AUTHOR

Robert Langs, M.D. is a classically trained psychoanalyst and program director of the Lenox Hill Hospital Psychotherapy Program. He is Editor-in-Chief of *The Yearbook of Psychoanalysis and Psychotherapy* and a practicing and supervising psychotherapist and psychoanalyst. Dr. Langs has written more than twenty books for the profession on aspects of psychoanalysis and psychotherapeutic technique and on studies of the therapeutic interaction. His work has specialized in studies of unconscious communication. Dr. Langs is also the founder of The Society for Psychoanalytic Psychotherapy and lectures widely in the United States and Europe.

OF RELATED INTEREST OF RELATED IN

MADNESS AND CURE

By Robert Langs, M.D.

A singular volume that will significantly revise your understanding of how psychotherapy works... and why it fails.

Can madness help cure madness? Therapist-madness – inappropriate defensive and frankly pathological behavior on the part of the therapist – is a major paradoxical factor in the symptom alleviation offered in present-day psychotherapies. Within every individual, whether patient or therapist, Dr. Langs maintains there is a core of madness ... terrifying in its content. Typically, therapist and patient engage in an unconscious collusion to avoid the anxiety of confronting and experiencing the truth of their respective madness.

But as harmful to patients as therapist-madness can be, particularly when manifested by assaultive interventions and sexual seduction, it can also be curative. Citing empirical data throughout, Langs describes the surprising mechanisms by which therapist-madness can lead to lasting patient relief. "Cure through sanity," is also defined. Langs demonstrates the salutary effects of "sane psychotherapy" and strongly advocates a resolution of the obstacles to its use posed by patients and therapists.

Madness and Cure is a creative and constructive attempt to identify unrecognized factors in the treatment experience and to clinically document their nature and influence. It will give the reader an entirely new understanding of how psychotherapy really works in today's world. Every therapist committed to truly sound psychotherapy will find this bold and revolutionary volume essential reading.

Partial Contents

ISBN 0-931231-05-1

NEWCONCEPT
press, inc.
EMERSON, NEW JERSEY